The Racial Cage

Forerunners: Ideas First

Short books of thought-in-process scholarship, where intense analysis, questioning, and speculation take the lead

FROM THE UNIVERSITY OF MINNESOTA PRESS

(Continued on page 89)

The Racial Cage

Nadine Ehlers, Anthony Ryan Hatch,
Amade Aouatef M'charek,
and Anne Pollock

University of Minnesota Press
MINNEAPOLIS
LONDON

ISBN 978-1-5179-1899-6 (PB)
ISBN 978-1-4529-7274-9 (Ebook)
ISBN 978-1-4529-7347-0 (Manifold)

Published by the University of Minnesota Press, 2025
111 Third Avenue South, Suite 290
Minneapolis, MN 55401-2520
www.upress.umn.edu

Available as a Manifold edition at manifold.umn.edu

The University of Minnesota is an equal-opportunity educator and employer.

Contents

Introduction

THE RACIAL CAGE is the result of a slow conversation about injustice, racism, health, and science that unfolded during the Covid-19 pandemic. Spurred by an endeavor we were involved in at the Sydney Centre for Healthy Societies at the University of Sydney, we gathered under the research theme "Race, Ethnicity, and the Biohumanities" to consider where it might conceptually take us and what political urgencies it might encompass. We have been both troubled and tantalized by the "biohumanities" part of this theme, but it proved productive for our conversations; it invited us to also open up that other concept in this theme: "race." The conversations that followed were particularly interesting given our similarities and differences: Each of us has been working independently on issues of race and drawing on STS scholarship in our ongoing research. We brought into our conversations different takes on race and ethnicity and different fields of research, from bioscience research to pharmaceuticals and medicine, from forensics to the governance of life, and from data to DNA. We brought our different domains of research and teaching to our effort to think and rethink the bio and the human, taking time to query each other's objects of study, methodological orientations, and epistemological commitments. We brought literary and interpretive as well as social science sensibilities to bear on our understandings of race, difference, and power, drawing insights from while working alongside the more established field of the medical humanities. As such, our conversations were always open-ended, never settling, and always leaving us with more questions.

Staying engaged within these virtual conversations across continents was perhaps possible in part because we already knew each other through multiple points of connection, through varied scholarly forums stretching back several years. The first time we all met in person was in September 2019, during a small and generative conference in London that was supported by a Small Grant from the Wellcome Trust on "Race and Biomedicine Beyond the Lab." Under ordinary circumstances our paths would probably have crossed again soon enough, but as it was, that we did so soon took intentionality. And so, with the aim of exploring race and the biohumanities, we scheduled virtual meetings for every few weeks as we worked from home amid ongoing lockdowns that were enforced to varying degrees, with the conversations taking place across great geographical distances—Australia, the United States, the United Kingdom, and the Netherlands—lending place-based specificities and complexities to our inquiries. After international travel became possible again, in early 2023 we convened for an in-person conference titled "Race, Health, and Asymmetries of the Human" at the University of Sydney and shared work-in-progress versions of the book's case studies. And the conversation continues.

Biohumanities

To begin thinking about the biohumanities and how it might relate to race, we first had to land on what we meant by race. We took it as a given that race is an unstable object and idea that eludes definition. Race might be seen as a set of knowledges applied to morphology, a discourse, what Stuart Hall called a "sliding signifier,"[1] but also

---

1. Stuart Hall, *The Fateful Triangle: Race, Ethnicity, Nation*, ed. Kobena Mercer, foreword by Henry Louis Gates, Jr. (Harvard University Press, 2017).

a set of practices: a formation, an enactment,[2] a material–semiotic relation.[3] We are interested here in the myriad things race can be and the ways race is made and remade in time and place.

With this in mind, we tentatively began to respond to other prompts that were fundamental, such as "what do you think that the biohumanities is?" and "how can the biohumanities be a response to the racial crisis of our time?" Ultimately, as we explain in more detail, the biohumanities, in our rendering, *takes as its object the multifaceted linkages between the "bio" and the "human,"* and it is also *a methodological lens that brings the biosciences and humanities into conversation* to open up the category of the human.

What possibilities does the concept of the biohumanities offer for making us think, for making us "look around," rather than ahead, as Anna Lowenhaupt Tsing would have it?[4] How could this concept move our thinking and inspire methodologies that help us attend to difference differently as well as to structural injustices? On the face of it, the combination of the bio and the human would seem to offer us more modernist trouble. Combining a biological rendering of the human with a humanist approach to what humans are seems to further solidify and naturalize a conception of universality. In what follows we take a theoretical step back and pause with some genealogical threads of the bio and the human and their relations with race, and then move on to consider the epistemological and methodological possibilities that the biohumanities enfolds.

---

2. See Nadine Ehlers, *Racial Imperatives: Discipline, Performativity, and Struggles Against Subjection* (University of Indiana Press, 2012); and Anthony Ryan Hatch, *Blood Sugar: Racial Pharmacology and Food Justice in America* (University of Minnesota Press, 2016).

3. See Amade M'charek, "Beyond Fact or Fiction: On the Materiality of Race in Practice," *Cultural Anthropology* 28, no. 3 (2013): 420–42; and Anne Pollock, *Medicating Race: Heart Disease and Durable Preoccupations with Difference* (Duke University Press, 2012).

4. Anna Lowenhaupt Tsing, *The Mushroom at the End of the World: On the Possibility of Life in Capitalist Ruins* (Princeton University Press, 2015).

In the formative *The Invention of Humanity*, the historian and political scientist Siep Stuurman shows how modernity and the modern states of justice are based on the (supposed) sameness of humans as the norm, and their (supposed) equality before the law is the consequence of this idea. He argues that historically there have been three crucial "modalities" that have helped invent this thing called humanity.[5] First, at the very earliest days of the Enlightenment in the eighteenth century, there is the acknowledgment of a common humanness, that is, the idea that humans belonged to the same biological species. The second modality is related to the anthropological turn of the late nineteenth and early twentieth centuries, through which cultural differences came to be understood as variation on a common theme, assuming a shared human culture. The third modality, contemporary with the anthropological turn, is a temporal regime that helped to think civilization in terms of an evolutionary development, in the way that even if some peoples are not there yet, they are assumed to undergo similar development and eventually arrive in modern times to come. Although the three modes that have helped establish the paradigm of humanity have been widely shared by different civilizations across the globe, so Stuurman argues, the coupling of equality and sameness became pivotal in racial Europe during the Enlightenment. The dictum was: To become equal is to become like those who are already equal, that is, the European whites. Enlightenment thus became the obligatory passage point for becoming equal.

As such, the concept of humanity, according to this reading, is inherently racial, and arguably racist. In addition, the modern, evolutionary biological concept of the human has contributed to what Chimamanda Ngozi Adichie has called "the danger of a single story":[6] a story that helps to order species, organisms, and related

5. Siep Stuurman, *The Invention of Humanity: Equality and Cultural Difference in World History* (Harvard University Press, 2017).

6. Chimamanda Ngozi Adichie, "The Danger of a Single Story," TEDGlobal, https://www.ted.com/talks/chimamanda_ngozi_adichie_the _danger_of_a_single_story, 2009.

entities on a line, that starts with the primordial soup to take us straight to the "now."[7] The biological and its rendering in the biological, life sciences, and medicine has been rightly critiqued for reductionist and essentializing gestures, and for contributing to the legitimization of inequalities, violence, and destruction. So, from this perspective it seems that juxtaposing the bio and the human gives us far more trouble rather than helping us attend to and intervene in such injustices. How have these stories been told? Why have they been so believable?

Intuitively in the twin figures bio-humanity, it is the bio that has been deemed fixed and rigid, the culprit of many harms and iniquities. But might it be that a different take on the bio could help decenter the human? Through this very juxtaposition, the bio helps us attend to the somatic aspects of the human, the fact that this human is situated in a body (that is not one, to evoke Annemarie Mol).[8] This way of thinking requires first that we accept that the biological cannot be reduced to a singular entity, be this an organism, cell, hormone, or gene. The biological is necessarily a nature-culture assemblage,[9] afforded through extended networks and practices. Second, precisely because the biological is relational and concerned with life (in its generality), it contributes to a decentering of the human. So, thinking this through, might the bio even radically shift the boundary between the human and the more than human, helping us look around, to touch and reconfigure our relations with the world? Might it help us address and rework injustices that do not only center on human relations but include our relations with more-than-humans/"earthbeings"?[10] Could the bio, precisely because it

7. Homi K. Bhabha, *The Location of Culture* (Routledge, 1994).

8. Annemarie Mol, *The Body Multiple: Ontology in Medical Practice* (Duke University Press, 2002).

9. Donna J. Haraway, *The Companion Species Manifesto: Dogs, People, and Significant Otherness* (Prickly Paradigm Press, 2003).

10. Marisol de la Cadena, *Earth Beings: Ecologies of Practice across Andean Worlds* (Duke University Press, 2015).

both recalls and decenters the human, help us attend to and rework ecological disasters and the way they are racially structured? Can the bio help us reimagine the ecological, including how social and political structures impinge on ecologies and multispecies lives?

This book engages and critiques the Enlightenment humanist story, where the human species has been seen as biologically hier-archized, with some positioned as more human than others, and where the human as ontological category has only been produced through (and thus depended on) the coproduction of marginalized nonpersonhood, animals, and objects (and the slippages between these). We critically examine this legacy by considering—as our *object* of analysis—the myriad linkages between the "bio" and the "human." In doing so, we eschew any simple understanding of the relationship between these two terms as simply referring to the biological properties of the human as species. As noted, this idea is infinitely fraught, as biology (and the sciences more generally) and the modern concept of "the human" have been essential to the division between humans, and between humans and nonhumans. Crucially, we also engage the linkages between bio and human, "biohumanities," as a *methodological lens* to open up the category of the human and thus to interrogate race.

What does a biohumanities approach entail? In one sense, the term has been invoked in philosophy and literature. Philosophers of science, for instance, have used the term *biohumanities* to char-acterize a mode of collaborative thinking that humanistic approach-es from philosophy and history of science can offer with/to/in/on biology itself.[11] For scholars of literature and medicine it has marked an enterprise that examines textual representations and interpretations of "biological, ecological, historical, and structural determinants of both the amelioration and the exacerbation of *suf-*

---

11. Karola Stotz and Paul E. Griffiths, "Biohumanities: Rethinking the Relationship Between Biosciences, Philosophy and History of Science, and Society," *The Quarterly Review of Biology* 83, no. 1 (2008): 37–45, https://doi.org/10.1086/529561.

fering."[12] While our rendering of biohumanities as a methodology takes aspects of these understandings into consideration, it is distinct in that it pursues a revised (posthuman) humanities approach. That is to say that our examination of culture and power in human societies (the traditional terrain of the humanities) is predicated on critically examining what we even mean by "human," rather than taking it as a given. But the biohumanities might offer both an approach or method and a *relationship*: studying the biosciences from a social and ethical perspective, while also bridging the ongoing conversations among biological and biomedical scientists on the one hand and humanities scholars on the other, and putting these often-disconnected domains into relation. Humanities can comment on the biosciences, but also add to the biosciences. Moving beyond a social determinants of health approach, biohumanities might offer a generative way to engage with how society and culture (including biology as a science) condition biological life.

Our vision of biohumanities brings the biosciences and their knowledges into the terrain of resources that we might use to interpret and reckon with our realities, past and present. This is not to elevate the biosciences above other forms of knowledge, nor is it to make biological knowledge subservient to other ways of knowing. Instead, we are interested in how bioscientific knowledges come about, as well as how they refract and reconfigure other forms of knowledge, and how this opens possibilities for new, generative analysis.

Specifically, we examine how *the figure of "human" contours biological life along lines of race,* and critically address *the politics that informs and conditions life*—at the level of embodied bio-materiality. We do so not to catalog "reality" (documenting what is happening) or arrive at "overarching meaning" (establishing veracity) but, rather, to highlight meaning-making practices and their effects.

12. Catherine Belling, "Introduction: From Bioethics and Humanities to Biohumanities?" *Literature and Medicine* 34, no. 1 (2016): 5.

Across its four chapters, this book theorizes the cage and caging as material–semiotic sites for racialization and for iteratively redefining the human–animal boundary.

Caging

As indicated previously, we brought our different fields of research into our conversations. We took the time to query each other's objects of research as methodological objects that could help us think and rethink the bio and the human. It is in this way that we came to the thematic of cages. Caging was pressing on our consciousness in different ways, ranging from living in lockdown in Sydney, to researching metabolism cages. We started to wonder whether cages and caging could be the overarching theme for us, a way into the puzzle of race, the biological, and the human, and a power relationship to explore, given how race and racism have long operated as caging mechanisms that contain and constrain. While the idea immediately captured something already at stake for some of us, others took time to think about how to give it content and contour in our contributions. We ended up bringing in literary and philosophical sensibilities to caging, race, and racism.

Under the social conditions of modernity and through the gaze of scientific racism that upheld those conditions, Europeans invented the modern concept of "race" to biologize the social and economic hierarchies that stratified human societies during and after colonialism. Conceptualizing race as biological—as located deep in the recesses of the body or written on its surface—created an ontological context where only white European men could be said to be fully human, with all others relegated to a beast-to-things continuum. Race became a way to think, act, and organize life in ways that registered and materialized social inequalities as biological and ascribed those inequalities to an essential animal(ized) nature, ostensibly caging non-whites within these knowledges. As a system of social power, racism, in turn, is deployed to cage those viewed as having "wild" bodies, recasting hierarchies of animality in distinctive racial formations. Race and species classifications delineate among the earth's creatures, by creating not only distances but also deep asymmetries that structure life chances, such as unequal patterns of health for human and nonhuman animals alike. Such asymmetries are inaugurated and sustained not only through practices of social closure and government but also through material artifacts that encircle and tame nonhuman animals' bodies and animalized human bodies for scientific, commercial, and political advantage. Empowered by policies and cultures organized around security, health, science, and leisure, the *practice of caging* enables certain peoples and creatures to be "kept." This book is concerned with the practices of caging related to racialized "others" (how caging functions as part of racialized social systems), and examines the ways caging draws on racial and species hierarchies for justification and meaning. Antiracist praxis must confront these cages, seeking to uncage their captives through inventive liberatory strategies of self-definition and collective mobilization.

In examining the concept of the cage and practices of caging, we look to critical race and ethnic studies, feminist studies, post-colonial sciences and technology studies, and their intersections to ask: How do science, technology, and medicine participate in the racial formation of metaphorical iron cages and real material cages? How is racism materialized through both metaphorical and literal cages? What critical ideas about biology, animality, and the human(ities) are needed to analyze how cages participate in racial formation, conditioned always by gender, class, sexuality, and geo-political factors?

What are we to make of the cage? Caging and then freeing oneself from the cage is the creative work of an escape artist. But usually, caged peoples are not magicians who orchestrate a performance of captivity, only to break through the chains, pick the locks, and flee the cage to escape mortal threat. While white-American figures like Henry Houdini popularized precisely that kind of performance escapology for white mass consumption in the twentieth century, Black figures like Henry Box Brown and Noble Drew Ali engaged in forms of escapology for political freedom and creative expression. Jacob Dorman tells the story of Noble Drew Ali, founder of the Moorish Science Temple in the 1910s, who advertised that he could free himself from bounded rope.[13] The abolitionist and performer Henry Box Brown packed himself into a shipping crate and shipped himself to freedom in 1849.[14] And Harriet Jacobs, as she describes in her autobiographical antebellum slave narrative *Incidents in the Life of a Slave Girl,* escaped into what she called a "loophole of retreat": a tiny crawl space above her grandmother's shed, where she hid for seven years to avert her master's persecution, remaining "hidden in plain sight."[15]

What has it meant for escapology to have emerged under the incantations of racecraft,[16] where we mistake the practice of escaping from cages as one that has nothing to do with escaping racism? And yet, performing and enacting even fraught forms of liberation offers practice for the real thing. For Christina Sharpe, the slave ship hull operates as a type of waterborne cage, ferrying Africans to the New World.[17] Yet caging might not be identical with enslavement while it is tactically involved in the act of enslaving others.

Critical race and ethnic studies scholars foreground that state officials have long used cages to confine people who are accused of

13. Jacob S. Dorman, *The Princess and the Prophet: The Secret History of Magic, Race, and Moorish Muslims in America* (Beacon Press, 2020).

14. See Daphne Brooks, *Bodies in Dissent: Spectacular Performances of Race and Freedom, 1850–1910* (Duke University Press, 2006); and Britt Rusert, *Fugitive Science: Empiricism and Freedom in Early African American Culture* (New York: New York University Press, 2017).

15. Harriet Jacobs, *Incidents in the Life of a Slave Girl* (Edgmont, 2022 [1861]).

16. See Karen E. Fields and Barbara J. Fields, *Racecraft: The Soul of Inequality in American Life* (Verso, 2014); Stephan Palmié, "Genomics, Divination, 'Racecraft,'" *American Ethnologist* 34, no. 2 (2007): 205–22; and Ruha Benjamin, "Conjuring Difference, Concealing Inequality: A Brief Tour of Racecraft," *Theory and Society* 43 (2014): 683–88.

17. Christina Sharpe, *In the Wake: On Blackness and Being* (Duke University Press, 2016).

committing violations of civil, criminal, and immigration laws. In the United States, there exists a long-standing practice of keeping detained migrants in cages and chain-link kennels, a racist policy that is supported by large segments of the citizenry. In 2019, the U.S. House of Representatives Committee on Oversight and Reform (Elijah Cummings, Maryland, Chairman) held a hearing titled "Kids in Cages: Inhumane Treatment at the Border," which was convened to draw critical attention to the practice.[18] Simultaneously, critical race and ethnic studies scholars have taken up the cage as a technology of state immigration policy and practice. Recent accounts of migrant children and families being kept in cages along the Mexico-- U.S. border have increased moral outrage, but as Sophia Jordán Wallace and Chris Zepeda-Millán point out, the original chain-link fences from World War II Japanese internment camps were dug out of the desert and repurposed to contain migrants and separate families along the border.[19] In Ana Minian's work, the United States represents a "cage of gold" that traps Mexican migrants who become a population without a country.[20]

In *Iron Cages,* Ronald Takaki describes the ideological forces in white culture that shape comparative attitudes and politics across racial and ethnic groups.[21] Mashing up the phrase from Parson's (mis)interpretation of Max Weber and Karl Marx, Takaki argues that racism forms part of an ideological superstructure, a kind of "iron cage" that culturally and materially organizes bodies, labor,

18. U.S. Government Publishing Office, "Kids in Cages: Inhumane Treatment at the Border," Hearing Before the Subcommittee on Civil Rights and Civil Liberties of the Committee on Oversight and Reform, House of Representatives, 116th Congress, July 10, 2019, https://www.congress.gov /event/116th-congress/house-event/LC64156/text?s=1&r=3.

19. Sophia Jordán Wallace and Chris Zepeda-Millán, *Walls, Cages and Family Separation: Race and Immigration in the Trump Era* (Cambridge University Press, 2020).

20. Ana Raquel Minian, "The Cage of Gold," in *Undocumented Lives. The Untold Story of Mexican Migration* (Harvard University Press, 2020).

21. Ronald Takaki, *Iron Cages: Race and Culture in 19th-Century America* (Oxford University Press, 2020 [1979]).

and power in Western capitalist societies. Cultural conditioning under what we now call racial capitalism leads to the mobilization of racist assumptions about the supposedly essential subhuman or nonhuman nature of non-whites.

These are just some of the ideas that inform—and unfold within—the chapters that follow. While the chapters here are each distinct, they developed in relation to one another and took shape through our shared conversations around the biohuman(ities), race, and the concept of caging.

Chapter 1 examines the metabolism cage—any scientifically engineered confinement system that captures and measures the flow of matter into and out of a confined animal's captive body. Metabolism cages emerged in the late eighteenth and nineteenth centuries as a key site for experiments in calorimetery throughout Europe, the United States, and their colonial and imperial satellites. It compares the racial discourses that keepers use to frame patterns of social inclusion and exclusion in metabolism cage research and to justify, interpret, and disseminate their scientific findings. The chapter narrates three stories. It opens with a story about Emil Osterberg, a Swedish-born custodian/scholar and known drinker, who was the first human to spend time in Wilbur Atwater's respiration calorimeter at Wesleyan University in the winter of 1896. The second story unfolds in the 1930s and tells the story of Jim—a Black man who worked as a "professional guinea pig" in William Abbott's research program at the University of Pennsylvania School of Medicine—and a bullet that was lodged in his body. The final story confronts the statistical correction for race and social difference in contemporary calorimetry, comparing differential access to high-tech metabolic cages, metabolic carts, and metabolic rooms used in intensive care units and clinical research facilities. It speculates that metabolism cages operate as racial cages because they are experimental spaces where conceptual ideas about race, human difference, and social inequality are forged and tested through scientific experiments and biomedical surveillance; they are commercial sites for the development of new technologies of economic exploitation, social stratification, and unequally distributed environmental harms; and they are dramaturgical sites where who gets to perform the role of keeper and who must play the role of the kept is structured by racial, gender, class, and species hierarchies.

Chapter 2 begins with the idea that, even though race is far from being caged in science and society, in social theory we tend to entertain limited views on what it is and thus cage it: For example, in the default statement, "race is not real, but is real in its consequences," or "race is a social construction." This chapter suggests that we ask the obvious yet overlooked question: "What is race *made to be in practice*"? Uncaging race is indeed a proposal for making space for this question, that is, to attend to race and study it more carefully so as to help demonstrate its presence in mundane practices that are seemingly indifferent to race. The chapter switches focus from race in relation to difference to race in relation to sameness, in order to attend to this question of what race is made to be in practice. Different modes of racialization based on sameness are explored: race as us-ness and race as otherness. Drawing on examples from a forensic DNA case as well as the public and political response to Europe's so-called refugee crisis, the chapter shows how racialization based on us-ness allows for variation and differentiation within the group, whereas racialization-based otherness tends to homogenize the group.

Chapter 3 engages with the ways the idea of the human contours biological life along lines of race, by examining two key quarantine technologies deployed in the racialized governance of health during the Covid-19 Delta lockdown in Sydney, Australia. The first of these technologies was a *caging* (or carceral control), applied in distinct and disparate ways across the population, such that some subjects were rendered lesser "humans," in line with the human/animal binary opposition of Western liberalism. The second technology was a staging (or spectacle) of minority spaces and residents, showing how race functions as a "cut" within the infrastructure of the state. The chapter explores how these technologies could be said to constitute a "zoological governance"—a form of governing relating to or affecting "lower animals" that does not exclude racialized subjects from the general populace, but instead pursues *conditional incorporation* to maintain racial reasoning and racial order.

Chapter 4 is concerned with not only naming what we don't want to see in the world but also what we do want to see. Continuing to examine the themes of carcerality and the boundaries of the human, this analysis shifts the focus to explore how the racial cage might have openings. First, the chapter considers the elusive and oppressive ideal of the hermetic seal in the context of Covid-19 and the vital breaking of the seal by the Movement for Black Lives. It then takes a more conceptual turn, considering the etymology and philosophy of "the cage" and the urgency of uncaging, as articulated in an earlier era by Marilyn Frye and Maya Angelou. In concluding our collective provocations around race, carcerality, and the biohumanities, this chapter closes with an insistence on refusing despair and holding on to necessary hope as we strive to dismantle cages of oppression.

We offer these chapters as kaleidoscopic reflections on the problematic of the racial cage. A kaleidoscope's glass and mirrors create changing patterns when the tube is rotated, and these chapters can do something analogous. They highlight constantly changing patterns or sequences of objects or elements of racial caging and linkages between the bio and human. Race cannot be looked at from one vantage point or single pattern of relations, and the chapters thus take diverse concrete entry points that are not precisely case studies. Drawn from different geographical contexts and pointed toward different objects and social relations, the illuminated fragments do not add up to a settled global view. They might be read in any order, but will be more interesting for being read together, refracting and diffracting distinct but interlinked articulations.

1. The Keepers and the Kept: Metabolism Cages in Racial Formations

Anthony Ryan Hatch

Metabolism Cages

The mental picture of a metabolism cage should not conjure an image of a circus-like barred cage or a wild animal trap. A metabolism cage is a scientifically engineered confinement technology that captures and measures the flow of matter into and out of a confined animal's captive body. Subject zero of metabolism cage research is the humble guinea pig whom Antoine Lavoisier, Marie-Anne Paulze Lavoisier, and Pierre Laplace placed into a rudimentary ice calorimeter in 1789.[1] The team wanted to discover how much heat from the animal was required to melt a given quantity of ice; this led to a scientific revolution in our understandings of respiration as a form of metabolic combustion in nature and in animal bodies. The Lavoisiers, for their part, were caught up in a political revolution—they were beheaded in the Reign of Terror during the French Revolution.

1. Ashworth E. Underwood, "Lavoisier and the History of Respiration," *Proceedings of the Royal Society of Medicine* 37, no. 6 (1944): 247–62.

Since 1789, dozens upon dozens of species of rodents, birds, primates, ruminants, and aquatic creatures have been kept inside metabolism cages for scientific, military, and commercial study. Mice, rats, guinea pigs, voles, squirrel, opossums, mink, hamsters, lemmings, beavers, manatees, rabbits, owls, chickens, turkeys, geese, fruit bats, lorikeets, llamas, deer, cows, yaks, goats, sheep, cats, dogs, pigs, seals, monkeys, and humans—they have all been kept inside metabolism cages. Therefore, this is not just one cage; there are hundreds of different cage designs of different sizes and capacities, each put into use in thousands of experiments designed to extract knowledge about how matter and bodies interact.

Metabolism formed as an object of biopolitical knowledge and target of institutional intervention mid- to late nineteenth century as new questions of labor, energy, and agriculture emerged under European colonialism and industrialization. The big question brought about through these relations of ruling was how to extract enough energy from nature to feed the dislocated, poor, and laboring masses in the colonies and metropoles enough to guard against revolutions and mass starvation.[2] New research programs at the intersection of comparative physiology and biological chemistry brought metabolism cages to bear on these complex new world problems. Well supported research programs at the University of Munich (Justus Leibeg, Carl Voit, Max Pettenkofer, Max Rubner), at Wesleyan University (Wilbur Atwater), and the Carnegie Nutrition Laboratory at Harvard (Francis Benedict), were exported elsewhere to help establish metabolism cages as an essential experimental apparatus around the world. While their use in experiments began in continental Europe and the Americas, they became a key part of transnational scientific infrastructures and colonial development projects throughout Africa, South America, Australia, and Asia.

2. Sheila Jasanoff, "Biotechnology and Empire: The Global Power of Seeds and Science," *Osiris* 21, no. 1 (2006): 273–92.

The so-called discovery of the calorie was made possible inside nineteenth-century metabolism cages.[3]

As part of a long-term, global effort to gather and operationalize vast amounts of intelligence about metabolism, metabolism cages feature in range of scientific fields including agriculture, nutrition, pharmacology, veterinary medicine, dairy and animal sciences, zoology, ecology, psychology, neuroscience, nuclear and sports medicine, environmental toxicology, weapons sciences, gnotobiotics, and space experiments. Humans sent metabolism cages to space aboard SpaceLab. The diversity of forms of matter that have been placed inside metabolism cages alone or passed through animals' bodies is all-encompassing of biotic and abiotic things. Flora, fauna, pharmaceuticals, toxins, cosmetics, ground up animal tissues, feces, TNT. If one can name a thing that might meet an animal during its life, it has likely been studied in a metabolism cage. What has come to be known in the biopharmaceutical and biochemical industries as ADME research (absorption, distribution, metabolism, excretion) must take place in metabolism cages because they are uniquely designed to capture bodies' material outputs in gas, solid, and liquid forms for study. The observable biochemical effects of any part of a molecule—a moiety—can be isolated inside metabolism cages.

For European and American scientists, metabolism operated as a metaphorical black box, a machine that transforms inputs into outputs through unknown and/or hidden mechanisms and transformations.[4] Knowing precisely what goes in and what comes out of metabolism cages tells scientists not only about the biochemical composition of the "inputs" and "outputs" but also about the bodies

3. Jane Dixon, "From the Imperial to the Empty Calorie: How Nutrition Relations Underpin Food Regime Transitions," *Agriculture and Human Values* 26, no. 4 (2009): 321–33.

4. Bruno Latour, *Pandora's Hope: Essays on the Reality of Science Studies* (Harvard University Press, 1999).

that process those the inputs into outputs.[5] To pose new questions about the metabolism of matter in caged animals, keepers had to devise new technoscientific instruments—metabolism cages—to capture the movements of matter through different kinds of plant and animal bodies. Opening the black box of metabolism required the development of new practices of instrumentation design and the integration of theories and methods needed to effectively contain different species.[6] Keeping different species in their own metabolism cages presented unique design challenges for cage designers and opened new epistemic frontiers for scientists and their institutional supporters in government and industry. Today, much of the so-named ADME research that takes place within metabolism cages today is carried out in service of commercial interests in the biochemical effects of food, drugs, and toxins. Multinational food and pharmaceutical companies have profited handsomely from the monetized knowledges that have accumulated by virtue of industrial scale animal confinement in metabolism cages.

"Respiratory calorimeters" were the first metabolism cages designed for humans in the so-called New World, along the lines of the famous apparatus that Wilbur Atwater and Edward Rosa built and operated at Wesleyan University from 1896 to 1908. With startup and operational funding from the university, local industry and private sponsors, and the United States Government, Atwater was able to maintain its expensive operational costs at $10,000 per year. Atwater and his colleagues conducted over five hundred experiments in this device; the ROI on this investment was favorable. As mentioned, this particular metabolism cage was used to

5. Frederic L. Holmes, "The Intake-Output Method of Quantification in Physiology," *Historical Studies in the Physical and Biological Sciences* 17, no. 2 (1987): 235–70.

6. J. A. McLean and Graham Tobin, *Animal and Human Calorimetry* (Cambridge University Press, 2007); Paul Webb, *Human Calorimeters* (Praeger, 1985).

establish and institutionalize the food calorie as a scientific mea-
surement of food's nutritive value.

Metabolism cages have been used profitably to "unlock" new
knowledges about how matter and bodies interact and this new
knowledge was acquired at the moral cost of mass scientific imprisonment of new world animals in metabolism cages. Despite
whatever intelligence metabolism cages have delivered to science,
nations, and industry, those benefits have been secured through
confinement. Scientific experiments involving metabolism cages
are premised on a simple carceral epistemology: a body in the cage
can be known, a body in the wild cannot be known.[7] The act of one
person keeping another animal in a metabolism cage establishes
a carceral relationship between the keeper and the kept. It is a
social and historical fact that some people have kept other people
and non-human animals inside metabolism cages in the name of
science and technological progress. Strangely, in accepted histories
of calorimetry, the practice of caging at the center of this science
is framed as incidental, peripheral, or altogether unrelated to the
core scientific questions and their epistemologies. This chapter
puzzles over the epistemological effects of carcerality on Western
metabolic knowledge, as evidenced in biomedical discourses comparing metabolism cage occupants as "free-living" or "in the wild,"
which I will discuss later.

Practices of segregation and aggregation take place at three "levels" of metabolism cage research: individual, pairs and small groups,
and social collectivities. The earliest metabolism cages were built
for keeping only one occupant, where that one individual occupant
stands in for or models its species, a population, or some other
scientifically meaningful group of which it is a members. Other
metabolism cages are designed for pairs or small groups of animals,
who are housed together strategically, often to reduce the stress of

7. M. J. Dauncey, "Whole-Body Calorimetry in Man and Animals,"
Thermochimica Acta 193 (1991): 1–40.

individual captivity on specimens. Metabolism cage designs can be institutionalized into the material infrastructure of social institutions and their pecuniary focus on the effects and distribution of food and drugs in prisons, labor camps, schools, and hospitals. Importantly, the intelligence derived from metabolism cage experiments involving humans was presumed to be universally applicable to all human beings—so-called "Man"—but that knowledge often had to be interpreted in terms of other social hierarchies linked to labor, race, gender, and age. Over time, ideas have changed about which species and persons should be kept in metabolism cages and what is to be learned from their confinement. Historically, the keepers have tended to be white male scientists with ties to state and industrial power. That hasn't changed much.

Historians of human and animal calorimetry have identified occupation, age, and gender as important social characteristics that metabolism cage researchers considered when calculating human energy needs, recruiting subjects, and securing funding for their work.[8] Within these histories, race is conspicuously absent from historical accounts of the scientific, design, and biomedical labor of human calorimetry, despite the emergence and persistence of extreme racial and ethnic inequalities in chronic metabolic disorders over the course of the twentieth century.[9] For humans, the most advanced metabolism cages for humans used today are mobile metabolic carts in intensive care units, metabolic rooms used in clinical research facilities, and portable calorimeters like Lumen, which

8. Elizabeth Neswald, "Food Fights: Human Experiments in Late Nineteenth-Century Nutrition Physiology," 95:170–93. *Clio Medica* (Brill, 2016).

9. James Doucet-Battle, *Sweetness in the Blood: Race, Risk, and Type 2 Diabetes* (University of Minnesota Press, 2021); Anthony Ryan Hatch, *Blood Sugar: Racial Pharmacology and Food Justice in Black America* (University of Minnesota Press, 2016); Michael Montoya, *Making the Mexican Diabetic: Race, Science, and the Genetics of Inequality* (University of California Press, 2011); Amy Moran-Thomas, *Traveling with Sugar: Chronicles of a Global Epidemic* (University of California Press, 2019).

are used by monied and metabolically curious Western consumers. These metabolism cages are experimental sites for the clinically consequential and highly controversial study of racial group differences in human metabolism. Articles, commentaries, and editorials in contemporary biomedical journals have been calling for the practice of race correction of the clinically significant biomarker: resting metabolic rate (RMR).[10] RMR refers to the amount of energy a body uses when it is "at rest"—awake, not eating, and not being active/exercising. Several widely used predictive equations such as Harris-Benedict (1918), Cunningham (1980), and Mifflin-St. Joer (1985) have been found to *overestimate* RMR in Black populations by up to three hundred calories per day, a miscalculation that leads to overfeeding critically ill patients in intensive care units. Human metabolism cages have helped identify these racially unequal mathematical practices in RMR estimation by cross validation—whole-body calorimeters are designed just for this purpose. I am curious how these calls are linked to the deeper social history of metabolism cages as sites for the production of scientific ideas about race and racial difference.

To make sense of this putatively racial cage, I develop a bio-humanities framework in this chapter, pairing social histories of racialized scientific labor and biocapital exchanged in human me-

---

10. Crystal C. Douglas et al., "Ability of the Harris-Benedict Formula to Predict Energy Requirements Differs with Weight History and Ethnicity," *Nutrition Research* 27, no. 4 (2007): 194–99; David Frankenfield et al., "Comparison of Predictive Equations for Resting Metabolic Rate in Healthy Nonobese and Obese Adults: A Systematic Review," *Journal of the American Dietetic Association* 105, no. 5 (2005): 775–89; B. A. Gower and L. A. Fowler, "Obesity in African-Americans: The Role of Physiology," *Journal of Internal Medicine* 288, no. 3 (2020): 295–304; James Reneau et al., "Do We Need Race-Specific Resting Metabolic Rate Prediction Equations?" *Nutrition & Diabetes* 9, no. 1 (2019): 21; Teresa A. Sharp et al., "Differences in Resting Metabolic Rate Between White and African-American Young Adults," *Obesity Research* 10, no. 8 (2002): 726–32; Christian Weyer et al., "Energy Metabolism in African Americans: Potential Risk Factors for Obesity," *The American Journal of Clinical Nutrition* 70, no. 1 (1999): 13–20.

tabolism cage research with a political analysis of who benefits from metabolism cage experiments. I open with the empirical question: Are metabolism cages sites of racial formation?[11] I hope to add to the very limited scholarship that is explicitly focused on the emergence of animal and human calorimetry and racial science.[12] To trace patterns of racial formation, I compare the racial (and often explicitly intersectional) discourses that keepers use to justify the patterns of racial inclusion and exclusion in metabolism cage research and to explain and interpret their scientific findings. I speculate that metabolism cages operate as racial cages because (a) they are experimental spaces where conceptual ideas about race, human difference, and social inequality are forged and tested through scientific experiments and biomedical surveillance; (b) they are commercial sites for the development of new technologies of economic exploitation, social stratification, and unequally distributed environmental harms; and (c) they are real dramaturgical sites where who gets to perform the role of keeper and who must play the role of the kept is structured by racial, gender, class, and species hierarchies.

The chapter continues with a short story about Emil Osterberg, a Swedish-born custodian/scholar and known drinker, who was the first human to spend time in Wilbur Atwater's respiration calorimeter at Wesleyan University in the winter of 1896. Perhaps it was his "Swedish-ness" that made him the ideal human subject zero for a metabolism cage. The second part of the chapter unfolds in the 1930s and tells the story of Jim—a Black man who worked as a "professional guinea pig" in William Abbott's research program at the University of Pennsylvania School of Medicine—and a bullet that was lodged in his body. Abbott was familiar enough with metabolism cages to joke about keeping Jim in one to get that bullet.

11. Michael Omi and Howard Winant, *Racial formation in the United States* (Routledge, 2014).

12. Warwick Anderson, *The Cultivation of Whiteness: Science, Health, and Racial Destiny in Australia* (Duke University Press, 2006).

These events surround the development of the Abbott-Miller Tube and highlight the evolving bioethics of race, gender, and class in experiments on commercially viable medical technologies linked to metabolism. The final section of the chapter addresses how historical practices of race correction shape contemporary inequalities in calorimetry, comparing differential access to high-tech metabolic cages and metabolic carts used in intensive care units and practices of race correction in the estimation of the resting metabolic rate.

A Sojourn in the Chamber

On February 17, 1896, Emil Osterberg, then a twenty-nine-year-old Swedish-born immigrant who worked as "a general assistant" for chemist Wilbur Atwater at Wesleyan University, became the first human being in the United States to voluntarily enter a human-sized metabolism cage. Osterberg became an assistant to Atwater, but his main gig was laboring as the custodian of Orange Judd Hall, where the device was located. Atwater and his colleague, Edward Rosa, built the apparatus they called a respiratory calorimeter, the first airtight metabolism cage built to hold one human at a time, and in its experiments, produced a wealth of knowledge about the food calorie and the biochemical substrates of human metabolism.

Emil's first experiment was in February 1896, but Atwater later enlisted him to participate in controversial alcohol experiments he conducted in the cage because "since boyhood, [Emil] was accustomed to the moderate use of alcoholic beverages."[13] Historians often elide Emil's first name for the substitution of his nationality (Bill Bryson called him "Swede Osterberg"[14] or Edward Kirkland

.

13. Wilbur O. Atwater, *Experiments on the Metabolism of Matter and Energy in the Human Body, 1898–1900* United States. Office of Experiment Stations. Bulletin; 109 (Government Printing Office, 1902), 2.
14. Bill Bryson, *The Body: A Guide for Occupants*. First United States edition (Doubleday, 2019).

who only offers his initial "E"[15]). In his write-ups of experiments, Atwater often took care to describe the nativity of his experimental subjects in terms of national or regional identities. Osterberg was "A Swede, by birth," Mr. A. W. Smith was "Canadian, by birth" and Dr. O. F. Tower was "a native of New England."[16] Osterberg participated in several cage experiments and even became a published author in the *American Journal of Physiology*. In 1900, he coauthored a paper with Francis Benedict (who went on to run the Carnegie Nutrition Laboratory that reported the results of their study placing human fat tissues biopsied from cadavers at the Connecticut Hospital for the Insane in Middletown into Atwater's smaller bomb calorimeter— "The Elementary Composition and Heat of Combustion of Human Fat.")[17] Perhaps Emil entered the cage a janitor and, through trials and tribulations, emerged a little-known scholar.

As human subject zero (in the U.S. context), Emil represented an ideal-type research subject for early human calorimeter researchers. Based on archival analysis, Elizabeth Neswald argues that the ideal subject for such studies was male, responsible, intelligent, and generally interested in the research; these qualities were needed to facilitate the research and endure the psychological pressures of being caged.[18] Only other Wesleyan-affiliated white male scientists and students participated in cage experiments during its twelve-year run in twenty-two or twenty-three experiments; I don't know how many Emil participated in. According to Kirkland, publishing magnate William Randolph Hearst once sent an unnamed "lady

15. Edward C. Kirkland, "'Scientific Eating': New Englanders Prepare and Promote a Reform, 1873–1907," *Proceedings of the Massachusetts Historical Society* 86 (1974): 28–52.

16. Atwater, *Experiments*, 239–40.

17. Francis Gano Benedict and Emil Osterberg, "The Elementary Composition and Heat of Combustion of Human Fat," *American Journal of Physiology-Legacy Content* 4, no. 2 (1900): 69–76.

18. "Food Fights: Human Experiments in Late Nineteenth-Century Nutrition Physiology," 95:170–93. *Clio Medica* (Brill, 2016).

reporter" to visit Atwater, demanding to spend time in the cage; Atwater was not happy with the stunt and did not allow it.[19]

Neswald's STS-inspired analysis raises questions about subjects' agency in human calorimeter research, framing the dynamic as one of resistance and cooperation, borrowing from Andrew Pickering's language.[20] Reading the brief published account of Emil's experience in the first experiment here, you can get a sense of Emil's apprehension and Wilbur's minimization of the "nervousness" of being sealed up in a cage. Also noteworthy are the elements of Emil's occupation, eating practices, and literacy that frame his participation.

> Respiration Experiment No. 1 (Digestion Experiment No. 11): The subject in this experiment was a Swede of 29 years of age who acted as a laboratory janitor and was accustomed to a moderate amount of muscular work. He would be called a hearty eater. During the progress of the experiments, he read a little for diversion, but the larger part of the time was as free from mental and physical activities as practicable. While he was entirely willing to do everything that was asked of him, it became evident that he did not find the sojourn in the chamber entirely agreeable. Toward the end of the second experiment he became somewhat ill, but the circumstances were such that it could hardly be attributed to any impure air or any other abnormal condition; indeed, there seemed to be good ground to believe that the slight illness was caused by nervousness due to the sojourn in the respiration chamber and an undefined and unfounded fear that some trouble might result.[21]

Emil worked in Judd Hall and did not sign up for this. According to this account, he did not have a good experience during his captivity in the chamber; "he did not find the sojourn in the chamber entirely agreeable," and by the end of his second experiment "he

19. Kirkland, "'Scientific Eating,'" 40.

20. Andrew Pickering, *The Mangle of Practice: Time, Agency, and Science* (University of Chicago Press, 1995).

21. Wilbur O. Atwater et al., *Report of Preliminary Investigations on the Metabolism of Nitrogen and Carbon in the Human Organism: With a Respiration Calorimeter of Special Construction.* United States. Office of Experiment Stations. Bulletin No. 44. (Government Printing Office, 1897), 40.

became somewhat ill." Clearly, he was willing to go in there but he freaked out. Maybe he gasped for air. What did it sound like in the chamber, as the gas pipes hissed and the light closed in around the singular window looking out into the basement? The scientific and economic promise in the device was too great for Atwater to be concerned with "undefined and unfounded fears" of being kept.

Jim's Bullet and the "Striking Blackamoors"

Jim was a Philadelphia-area Black man who became involved in the research program of William Osler Abbott, a gastroenterologist who arrived at the University of Pennsylvania School of Medicine in 1930–31, joining the research lab of Dr. T. Grier Miller. Having been trained in the nascent fields of pharmacology and physiology, Abbott's specific interest in gastroenterology was developing new devices and techniques to deliver drugs into the body. In Dr. Miller's words, Abbott "wished to carry over to human beings [from other species] certain experiments on the motor effects of various drugs on the duodenum."[22] Over a twelve-year period, Abbott conducted five hundred intestinal intubation experiments including tests on himself, as was common practice at the time among research physicians.

In 1957, the austere outlet *Transactions of the American Clinical and Climatological Association* published a speech Abbott delivered in 1939 before *The Charaka Club,* a group of doctors who shared an interest in literature, in a dark world cast of medical humanities.[23] Titled "The Problem of the Professional Guinea Pig,"

22. Grier T. Miller, "Development of the Double-Lumened Tube for Intestinal Intubation," *Journal of the American Medical Association* 140, no. 2 (May 1949): 147–49, 147.
23. Osler W. Abbott, "The Problem of the Professional Guinea Pig," *Transactions of the American Clinical and Climatological Association* 68 (1957): 1–9.

Abbott's speech describes his ethically fraught and logistically troubled efforts going back to 1931 and over the course of the Great Depression to manage a pool of human recruits in his experiments of a rapid mouth-to-anus gastrointestinal tube and its accompanying techniques. In Abbott's view, the people whom he experiments upon are the "professional guinea pigs" who take the job because it pays during a time when little else does. Pay could be upward of two dollars a day (about thirty-eight in today's dollars).

Jim, along with a small group of Philadelphia-area Black men, was a professional guinea pig in several of Abbott's studies, which often involved subjects swallowing rubber tubing up to twelve feet in length and repeated x-ray exposures. During a Black-men-only phase of his research program, Abbott jokes that there were "mishaps." One such event revolved around an anecdote he narrates about Jim:

> I once attempted to manipulate a tube quickly into Jim's duodenum by fluoroscopic guidance when my eyes were not well accommodated. After a good deal of vigorous palpation, I suddenly realized that the metal tip which I had been struggling to direct was behind Jim's spinal column. A cold rivulet of perspiration trickled down my own spine. Then my eyes, by that time used to the dim light, detected an unfamiliar contour to the "bucket" and it dawned on me that what I had been trying to manipulate with notably small success was a .38 calibre revolver bullet in his erector spinae muscles. When confronted with the evidence, Jim grinned sheepishly and admitted that he'd made a grave error the night before. He had called on his sweetheart unaware of the fact that she had seen him that very evening with another girl. Such events led me to wish at times that I could keep my animals in metabolism cages.[24]

Historians of medicine are also familiar with Abbott's discourse and have interpreted this last sentence as evidence of Abbott's use of violent and exploitative rhetoric and cultural racism given how he animalized Black men to justify an ethically fraught research

24. Abbott, "The Problem," 3–4.

program.[25] In my reading, the only reason why he would joke that he wanted to keep his animals (like Jim) in metabolism cages would be to avoid having to go through Jim's feces by hand later to fish the bullet out himself. I think what Abbott really wanted was a keepsake.

Abbott's positions on the animality of blackness in the context of metabolism cage research make sense given his broader views about animals and humans in medical experimentations. Abbott's use of animalizing discourse is evidenced throughout the speech, along with glib efforts at humor, a boring doctor's wit, and self-serving social commentary. As you can read here in the opening paragraph, "It is then to the problem of the capture, selection, care, and training of good, healthy human guinea pigs, if I may use a trite phrase, that I would invite your attention." Another example: "We had a metaphorical can opener but no beef, and beef we were determined to have."[26] In this couplet, the tube device is the can opener and the human subjects are the "beef." Abbott's view was that a wide variety of humans should work as professional guinea pigs because "If the proper study of mankind is man, then there can be but one really satisfactory experimental animal."[27] Yet, he also discusses the scientific rationale and practical exigencies of studying different species for different reasons, partly due to the specificities of the question at hand: "In this way, a student can study the effect of the procedure on the animal that really matters."[28] If the question is about humans, study humans. If the question is about dogs, study dogs.

25. Susan E. Lederer, *Subjected to Science: Human Experimentation in America before the Second World War* (Johns Hopkins University Press, 1995); Harriet A. Washington, *Medical Apartheid: The Dark History of Medical Experimentation on Black Americans from Colonial Times to the Present*, 1st ed. (Doubleday, 2006); T. G. Schnabel Jr., "William Osler Abbott: His Double Lumen Tube," *Transactions of the American Clinical and Climatological Association* 112 (2001): 50–60.

26. Abbott, "The Problem," 2.

27. Abbott, 1.

28. Abbott, 8.

Upon the suggestion of his secretary, Abbott enlists his Black custodian (yes, another custodian), Harry, to help him recruit a group of Black men ("apparently sober and in a state of fasting at 8:30 am") for the studies, which he does. Flip, Sam, Dan, Slim, Dan, and unnamed others appear. Abbott recounts one occasion when the group collectively refused to show up for a scheduled public intubation at the American Medical Association unless Abbott doubled their pay, which was currently $1.50 per hour. Using the racial epithet "blackamoors" to describe this group, Abbott recounts their collective labor action against him and how he managed it:

> Had I been an older hand at the role of captain of industry, I would have foreseen it, but as it was, I had no inkling of what was brewing until a certain day less than a week before the convention when the whole crowd went on strike together. Double the pay or no demonstration was the demand. That was a bad few minutes for me. No dogs, cats, rats or rabbits that I had ever handled had done this, but there was one opening left. It was then 1:30 P.M. At 2:00 the last examination of the spring term, third year obstetrics, was due to begin. I left the black delegation sitting and sprinted for the Medical School. As the students gathered, I gave them an impassioned appeal for volunteers, offered the pay of my *striking blackamoors,* and in five minutes a shipment of scab labor had signed up, that would have made any factory foreman green with envy. Thereupon I returned to the committee, and, the National Labor Relations Board being as yet unborn, I had the pleasure of indulging in a little old-fashioned capitalism. We fired the whole lot of them, lock, stock and barrel. The exhibit went off like clockwork. The volunteers from the third year class stood up to those tubes like veterans of the line.[29]

In addition to remarking on the need to expand the experiments conducted on people living in asylums and prisons, upon his wife's suggestion Abbott started recruiting in the local papers, drawing in the city's poor and working-class people, including many women, into his research program. For Abbott, within each respective species there is an identifiable segment of the population that is more amenable to experimentation given variations in "tempera

29. Abbott, 4.

ment," which is "governed by a set of natural laws which are fairly universal." Differences in temperament generate two groups: the ones that fight and refuse and what he calls "the ones that stick." He explains the difference in a direct comparison between dog and human recruits:

> Were one doing a chronic experiment on a dog, say a long-time absorption problem with a Thirey fistula, he would not go to the animal house and pick a wiry young bull pup with hair-trigger nervous system and a desire to fight everything in sight. Obviously, one would pick a big, lazy, overweight bitch that could be counted upon to lie and wag her tail while being worked over, and, interestingly enough, it is always to the human counterpart of this animal that my clientele dwindles down. Each year the lean ones seem to have strayed away from me, the younger ones have better jobs and the newlyweds are having another baby or have moved away, but the easy-going hundred forty-pounders with a streak of gray beginning to show, bring their knitting and their children's photographs and pair off in congenial couples so they can gossip the tedium as the tubes go down. They are the ones that stick.[30]

For Abbott, the best experimental subject was one whose body is inured to the violence of fatness, laziness, debauchery, complacency—all cultural stereotypes about Black, poor, and working-class people in Depression-era Philadelphia.

Miller and Abbott would go on to coinvent the Miller-Abbott Tube in 1939, a double-lumen rubber tube featuring an opening to the stomach for suction, another opening to the jejunum for feeding, and on the other end a small balloon filled with mercury (to aid gravity in passing the tube). Until 1978, the Miller-Abbott Tube was widely used to intubate the gastrointestinal tract and break obstructions, deliver drugs and enteral nutrition beyond the stomach. It fell out of use due to complications with the mercury and the emergence of superior designs.[31] Still, Abbott made "contributions" to enteral

---

30. Abbott, 8.
31. Laura Harkness, "The History of Enteral Nutrition Therapy: From Raw Eggs and Nasal Tubes to Purified Amino Acids and Early Postoperative

medicine, involving serious medical situations in which knowing precisely how much food to push into a body means life or death.

Race Correction in Calorimetry

Critically ill, immobilized, and unconscious human bodies still must receive calories (and other nutrients) from food, even if they are unable to chew or swallow raw or prepared foods. Guided by legal standards of care and financial arrangements, medical providers and pharmacists administer nutrition enterally, or via tubes, to patients in wide variety of precarious medical situations.[32] This branch of clinical nutrition is called enteral nutrition. Standard histories of tube feeding in medicine often minimize this practice, which is genealogically linked to the punitive practice of force-feeding feminist revolutionaries, prisoners, and asylum residents. Enteral feeding is difficult to get right, is painful, and can lead to its own medical complications. Comparative outcome research conducted demonstrates that underfeeding and overfeeding people in these situations can be harmful to an already traumatized and recovering body. Additionally, the kinds of traumas that befall a critically ill patient have direct and observable metabolic consequences on their own, effects that medical providers must account for when providing emergency care. So, how do doctors figure out what and how much to feed immobilized human bodies while avoiding consequences and improving critical care outcomes for these patients? The answer has to do with calculating precisely how much energy is required for that body to function when it is at rest (this is called the resting metabolic rate, or RMR), while accounting for other situational factors.

Jejunal Delivery," *Journal of the American Dietetic Association* 102, no. 3 (2002): 399–404.

    32. Elaine J. Amella et al., "Tube Feeding: Prolonging Life or Death in Vulnerable Populations?" *Mortality* 10, no. 1 (2005): 69–81.

In practice, there are two ways to calculate RMR. The first and best approach, considered the gold standard, involves keeping a patient's body within one of two types of contemporary metabolism cages: a metabolic room or a portable metabolic cart, both of which allow clinicians to indirectly calculate the RMR.[33] Metabolic carts and metabolic rooms are used in clinical research facilities and intensive care units (ICUs) and are high-tech descendants of Atwater's late Victorian respiratory calorimeter. Strangely, these are metabolism cages a person might want to be kept in for a brief period, should they be in the unfortunate situation where they cannot take food by mouth, so that medical providers can get the numbers right. The number of large, whole-body human calorimeters that have been built around the world is somewhere north of three dozen while the number in full operation today is smaller and clustered in the Global North (especially in the United States and Europe). Metabolism cages are expensive pieces of technical equipment that have sited significant biomedical and environmental research. Especially since the 1980s, this research has been justified within a health inequalities frame, recruiting the kept based on their membership in social groups experiencing health disparities.

The second approach is exclusively mathematical in which the patient's anthropometric characteristics are entered into an algorithm or equation that estimates resting metabolic rate (RMR) in comparison to population-level parameters. Unfortunately, the numeral standards for human RMR were established in 1915 in exclusively white and presumed homogeneous reference populations.[34] Analysts are calling for RMR estimations to undergo some form of "race correction" that accounts for the assumption of racial differences in RMR. This is different from the eGFR case of race

33. H. Mtaweh et al., "Indirect Calorimetry: History, Technology, and Application," *Frontiers in Pediatrics* 6, no. 257 (n.d.).

34. Frank C. Gephart and Eugene F. DuBois, "Fourth Paper: The Determination of the Basal Metabolism of Normal Men and the Effect of Food," *Archives of Internal Medicine* 15, no. 5 (1915): 835–67.

correction as articulated by Lundy Braun and Dorothy Roberts because, unlike that case in which race is explicitly included, "race is not considered in formulas used to determine caloric requirements in clinical practice."[35]

In *Nutrition & Diabetes,* researchers ask, "Do We Need Race-Specific Resting Metabolic Rate Equations?"[36] This question is raised in a context where Black patients do not have equal access to the best enteral nutrition across the life course including Black infants, children, and adults in critical care situations and Black elders in end-of-life scenarios where feeding tubes are often used to provide nutritional and pain support.[37] Given these racial inequalities, how do the mathematical versus technological measurements of RMR compare in terms of how intersectional inequalities are surveilled, represented, and explained? Should race be considered in RMR estimations and if so, how?

In the 1990s and 2000s, several studies observed race and gender differences in RMR as measured via indirect calorimetry in metabolism cages.[38] During this period, researchers posited genetic theories to explain these social differences, featuring comparisons

35. James Reneau et al., "Do We Need Race-Specific Resting Metabolic Rate Prediction Equations?" *Nutrition & Diabetes* 9, no. 1 (2019): 5.

36. Reneau et al., "Do We Need," 21.

37. Ayham Khrais et al., "Trends Regarding Racial Disparities Among Malnourished Patients with Percutaneous Endoscopic Gastrostomy (PEG) Tubes," *Cureus* 14, no. 11 (2022): e31781; Howard B. Degenholtz et al., "Race and the Intensive Care Unit: Disparities and Preferences for End-of-Life Care," *Critical Care Medicine* 31, no. 5 (2003): S373; Nan Tracy Zheng et al., "Racial Disparities in In-Hospital Death and Hospice Use Among Nursing Home Residents at the End-of-Life," *Medical Care* 49, no. 11 (2011): 992–98.

38. Dympna Gallagher et al., "Small Organs with a High Metabolic Rate Explain Lower Resting Energy Expenditure in African American than in White Adults," *The American Journal of Clinical Nutrition* 83, no. 5 (2006): 1062–67; T. M. Manini et al., "European Ancestry and Resting Metabolic Rate in Older African Americans," *European Journal of Clinical Nutrition* 65, no. 6 (2011): 663–67; Christian Weyer et al., "Energy Metabolism in African Americans: Potential Risk Factors for Obesity," *The American Journal of Clinical Nutrition* 70, no. 1 (1999): 13–20.

of ancestral informative markers (AIM) and measurements of racial admixture.[39] Researchers also offered physiological explanations for African Americans' comparatively lower RMR compared to Whites: RMR is related to European ancestry via selective pressures on mitochondria that advantaged populations who lived in "higher latitudes"[40] and RMR is lower in African Americans because of group differences in the fractional mass of high metabolic rate organs (e.g., brain, liver, kidney).[41] Within this logic of scientific racism, Gower and Fowler argue that "race can be deconstructed into physiologic variables that explain free-living gain in body fat" based upon the presumption that all Black people have "inherently high AIRg (Acute Insulin Response to glucose)."[42]

Questions of how the variables of race and gender effect differential outcomes frame the overarching research program, leading to sampling frameworks that specifically feature enough Black men and women to permit statistical comparisons to white men and women. In this period, analysts focused on explaining high rates of obesity and susceptibility among Black girls, adult premenopausal and overweight Black women, and older "free-living" Black women.[43] Any racial and/or ethnic differences that were identified in a sample

39. Jose R. Fernandez et al., "Association of African Genetic Admixture with Resting Metabolic Rate and Obesity Among Women," *Obesity Research* 11, no. 7 (2003): 904–11.

40. Manini et al., "European Ancestry."

41. Gallagher et al., "Small Organs"; Fahad Javed et al., "Brain and High Metabolic Rate Organ Mass: Contributions to Resting Energy Expenditure Beyond Fat-Free Mass," *The American Journal of Clinical Nutrition* 91, no. 4 (2010): 907–12.

42. B. A. Gower, and L. A. Fowler, "Obesity in African-Americans: The Role of Physiology," *Journal of Internal Medicine* 288, no. 3 (2020): 295–304.

43. Jeanine B. Albu et al., "Visceral Fat and Race-Dependent Health Risks in Obese Nondiabetic Premenopausal Women," *Diabetes* 46, no. 3 (1997): 456–62; William H. Carpenter et al., "Total Daily Energy Expenditure in Free-Living Older African-Americans and Caucasians," *American Journal of Physiology-Endocrinology and Metabolism* 274, no. 1 (1998): E96–101; Susan Zelitch Yanovski et al., "Resting Metabolic Rate in African-American and Caucasian Girls," *Obesity Research* 5, no. 4 (1997): 321–25.

could not be interpreted independently from gender. Carpenter and colleagues proclaimed to be the first group to examine "the effects of race on daily energy expenditure in free-living African Americans," drawing a clear distinction with research that takes place inside an unfree experimental place like a metabolism cage.

Among the sites where such comparative racial research has taken place is within the Clinical Diabetes and Nutrition Section at the U.S. National Institutes of Health complex in Phoenix, Arizona in the 1980–1985 period, led by Eric Ravussin.[44] This facility featured a then-state-of-the-art respiratory chamber modeled after one built at the University of Lausanne in Switzerland in the 1970s, where Ravussin earned his PhD in human physiology. In justifying their approach to using indirect calorimetry via this particular metabolism cage to study Black women's propensity for obesity, Weyer and colleagues argued that the prior studies showing Black women to have a lower resting metabolic rate than white women were flawed because they were not conducted over a long enough period of time and they were conducted using "ventilated-hood systems."[45] In contrast to what was known about Black women, "little is known about energy metabolism in African American men," they assert. To study these (intersectional) dynamics, their objective was to compare twenty-four-hour measurements of energy metabolism between African American and white women and men using a respiratory chamber. They found "ethnic differences" in sleeping metabolic rate (SMR), twenty-four-hour respiratory quotient (24RQ), and fat-free mass (single best determinant of energy expenditure). The "ethnic differences in energy metabolism seem to be sex specific, i.e., energy expenditure was lower particularly in African American women, whereas in men, the major ethnic difference was in substrate oxida-

44. E. Ravussin et al., "Determinants of 24-Hour Energy Expenditure in Man. Methods and Results Using a Respiratory Chamber," *Journal of Clinical Investigation* 78, no. 6 (1986): 1568–78.

45. Weyer et al., "Energy Metabolism," 16.

tion."[46] They also found ethnic differences in body fat distribution and body composition as measured by fat-free mass, which Weyer and colleagues describe as "the single best determinant of energy expenditure in humans."

Importantly, Eric Ravussin and his colleagues took up the question of how the knowledge derived from studies of human metabolism that take place in the cage relates to knowledge derived from studies that take place among "free, living" individuals.[47] One of the big differences between being in a cage and not is the movement of the body in space, what the researchers refer to as "spontaneous physical activity" or SPA. Snitker and colleagues studied this question in fifty nondiabetic Pima Indians, who completed a twenty-four-hour stay in the Arizona respiratory chamber followed by a seven-day follow-up of "free-living" using the doubly labeled water method of indirect calorimetry, which involves "enriching the body water of a subject with heavy oxygen and heavy hydrogen and then determining the difference in washout kinetics between both isotopes."[48] The doubly labeled water method "has proved an ideal technique for the estimation of 'field' metabolic rate in free-living animals and birds."[49] This technique, first developed by Lifson and McClintock, which does not require caging, has been widely adopted to study energy needs in free-living animals.[50]

46. Weyer et al., 16.

47. S. Snitker et al., "Spontaneous Physical Activity in a Respiratory Chamber Is Correlated to Habitual Physical Activity," *International Journal of Obesity* 25, no. 10 (2001): 1481–86.

48. Klaas R. Westerterp, "Doubly Labelled Water Assessment of Energy Expenditure: Principle, Practice, and Promise," *European Journal of Applied Physiology* 117, no. 7 (2017): 1277–85, 1279.

49. Dauncey, "Whole-Body Calorimetry," 10.

50. N. Lifson and Ruth McClintock, "Theory of Use of the Turnover Rates of Body Water for Measuring Energy and Material Balance," *Journal of Theoretical Biology* 12, no. 1 (1966): 46–74; International Atomic Energy Agency, *Assessment of Body Composition and Total Energy Expenditure in Humans Using Stable Isotope Techniques* (International Atomic Energy Agency, 2009).

The Keepers and the Kept

Who benefits from metabolism cage research? The keepers or the kept? Much of what is known about metabolism was studied under experimental conditions involving multispecies confinement in metabolism cages; this knowledge has been used to engineer new genres of foods, drugs, toxins, and weapons. This account of the racialized scientific labor involved in conducing metabolism cage research and analysis of the multiple forms of biocapital exchanged in that research both point to complex racial meanings and social structures that are linked to the production of knowledge about race and animal metabolism. In this way, metabolism cages are an example of what Thomas Gieryn calls a truth spot where how we know what we know about animal metabolism is sanctioned, encultured, and instrumentalized to build an industrialized and carceral form of metabolism.[51] In order for the metabolism cage as truth spot to function properly, a political drama must play out; somebody must play the role of the keeper and somebody else has to be kept.

This carceral relationship between the keepers and the kept maps onto a scientific relationship between scientist experimenters and their specimen(s). Dr. Abbott plays the keeper and Jim, one of his animals, gets inside the cage so Abbott doesn't have to go through his feces by hand. Dr. Atwater plays the keeper and Emil, his building's janitor, gets inside the cage and takes a drink to calm his fears of captivity and suffocation. Dr. Ravussin plays the keeper and his racialized patients with serious metabolic disorders get inside the cage so that scientists can evidence claims about asocial biological differences within a broader discourse about the universal human. Identifying, assembling, and evaluat-

51. Thomas F. Gieryn, *Truth-Spots: How Places Make People Believe* (University of Chicago Press, 2019).

ing evidence about the historical, multinational, and multisector costs and benefits of metabolism cage research is a daunting empirical task given the industrial scale of the enterprise. Any analysis of who benefits from this form of mass scientific imprisonment and data extraction that does not take carcerality itself or racism into account is limited by virtue of its attempted separation of the biological and the human.

2. Uncaging Race: A Proposal for Curiosity and Care for Wild Objects

Amade Aouatef M'charek

By Way of Introduction: Curiosity, Care, and Sameness

The title of this chapter, "uncaging race," might evoke some thoughts. One obvious thought would be that we are dealing with something dangerous and wild. And so we are. But it might also suggest that since race is dangerous and caged, we know what it is. Adding to this, precisely because race is caged, we are aware of its politics, and we therefore want to confine its place in science and society. Perhaps caging has been a politics of exorcising the power of race, a way of taming its malicious political effects.

But perhaps this caging has also limited our modes of knowing race, and our capacity to be curious about it—such as raising the obvious yet overlooked question: What is race? One conventional answer would be that race is a biological difference between groups of people, a fact (supposedly), to be found on, or deep down in the body. Another way to answer to this question would be that race is not biology but, rather, a social construction, located in our ideologies, infrastructures, and institutions. One could say that these are the two default answers to what is race, of which the second is taken to be the most relevant answer. But precisely the default nature of these answers has prevented us from pausing with race and from being *seriously curious* about it. I mobilized the notion of curiosity on purpose here, not as a moral appeal but as a methodological call to slow down and open up toward this troubling object that is everywhere and nowhere. I am drawing on Michel Foucault's call to appreciate curiosity in research practices. He says:

> Curiosity is a vice that has been stigmatized in turn by Christianity, by philosophy, and even by a certain conception of science. . . . However, I like the word. . . . It evokes "care"; it evokes the care one takes of what exists and what might exist; a sharpened sense of reality, but one that is never immobilized before it; a readiness to find what surrounds us strange and odd; a certain determination to throw off familiar ways of thought and to look at the same things in a different way; a passion for seizing what is happening now and what is disappearing; a lack of respect for the traditional hierarchies of what is important and fundamental.[1]

Foucault points out that curiosity and care are part of a family of resemblance; they have common etymological roots. French and Latin roots connect curiosity—via *curiositas, curiosus,* and *cura*—to desire for knowledge, to being careful, and to care. One could thus say that to be curious about race is to care for race.

Now, caring might come easy or feel good when it is directed toward something that we value as a good. Caring for the environment or biodiversity, or for humanity seems like a politically good thing to do. But how do we care for something as threatening and ugly as race? How do we care for something that has caused so much harm and disasters? And, in a more complicated sense, how do we care for something that is illusive and slippery, something that keeps shifting shape and content, or comes in coded language?[2]

---

1. Christian Delacampagne, "The Masked Philosopher," in *Michel Foucault, Ethics: Subjectivity and Truth, Essential Works of Foucault (1954–1984)* 1 (1990 [1980]). http://1libertaire.free.fr/MFoucault189.html.

2. See Stuart Hall, "Minimal Selves," in *The Real Me: Post Modernism and the Question of Identity*, ed. Lisa Appignanesi (ICA Document 6). (The Institute of Contemporary Arts, 1980), 44–46; see also David Skinner,

Perhaps the clue is to shift focus, from caring for the object (race) to caring for our modes of relating to it (methods).[3] Crucially, here, is the idea that curiosity and care also share an ethos of relating to the object of inquiry or the object of attention. To know, as well as to care, is to enter into a relation, one that is not goal directed but open-ended; a relation that involves "tinkering" and the making of space for the unexpected.[4] To be clear, my point is not that we should love race. Rather, I want to engage in being curious about it by shifting attention to how we study it. What horizons emerge if we decide that we do not know what it is beforehand, but, rather, keep asking the question: What is it made to be in different practices? In this chapter I explore how we can know race differently by methodologically switching focus: from attending to race through the lens of *difference,* to a mode of understanding it through the lens of *sameness.* Now, for obvious reasons we have developed an alertness to the politics of difference, especially in relation to race. While difference for the elite might come with privileges and distinctions, for the large groups in society it has often come with stigmatization, exclusion, and violence. Yet, the focus on the politics of difference has also sustained the idea that when it comes to race, differences are political as they are made and can be unmade, while similarities are assumedly given and apolitical.

The idea that similarities are given and the fact that we take them for granted in everyday life might actually have deeper, more structural roots. We have alluded to this in the introduction to this book through the reference to the Dutch historian Siep Stuurman. For Stuurman, modernity and modern states are built on the idea of the sameness of humans as the norm, and their (supposed) equality

"Racialized Futures: Biologism and the Changing Politics of Identity," *Social Studies of Science* 36, no. 3 (2006): 459–88.

3. For an elaboration on this argument, see Amade M'charek, "Curious About Race: Generous Methods and Modes of Knowing in Practice," *Social Studies of Science* 53, no. 6 (2023): 826–49.

4. Annemarie Mol et al., eds., *Care in Practice: On Tinkering in Clinics, Homes and Farms* (transcript Verlag, 2010).

before the law is its consequence.[5] As elaborated in the introduction, Stuurman argues that the coupling of equality and sameness as
an aspiration during the early Enlightenment has become pivotal in
racial Europe. In an evolutionary approach, in which the culturally
backward other will eventually become more civilized, enlightenment became the obligatory point of passage for becoming equal.
As a consequence, sameness became the *normative baseline* of this
modern equality paradigm.

Crucially, for us here, is the reality that sameness is not given but
made and that it is racialized. In what follows I explore how the lens
of sameness can help us explore specificities of how race is done in
practice, by distinguishing between two modes of doing sameness:
sameness in relation to *otherness* and sameness in relation *us-ness.*
One could say that these different dynamics of doing sameness produce different versions of the biohuman. Especially since the racialization of sameness, as I will show, necessarily incorporates aspects
of the body and the biological, the bio and the human get conjured
up in a normative "nature-culture assemblage."[6] I will draw on two
examples, a forensic homicide case, and a series of responses to
what is called "Europe's refugee crisis," to demonstrate how sameness is done and what version of race it helps produce. While my
work usually focuses on scientific practices, in this chapter I draw
on examples from media outlets and related venues for my analyses.

Doing Race and Sameness in a Dutch Homicide Case

My first example comes from a Dutch homicide case related to the
murder of Marianne Vaatstra.[7] This high-profile forensic case in fact

5. Siep Stuurman, *The Invention of Humanity: Equality and Cultural
Difference in World History* (Harvard University Press, 2017).

6. Donna Jeanne Haraway, *The Companion Species Manifesto: Dogs,
People, and Significant Otherness,* vol. 1 (Prickly Paradigm Press, 2003).

7. I here draw on Amade M'charek, "Race and Sameness: On
the Limits of Beyond Race and the Art of Staying with the Trouble,"
Comparative Migration Studies 10, no. 1 (2022): 1–16.

alerted me to the issue of sameness and race, as I will elaborate in the following section. It took almost thirteen years to resolve the case, a time during which the case remained open, almost without interruption. Over the years I have followed the case closely, as it provoked a number of legislative changes geared toward the use of an increasing number of novel forensic DNA technologies in the hope of resolving the case. This eventually happened in November 2012, through a so-called DNA dragnet focused on familial searching.

A Non-Dutch Manner of Death: On Sameness as Otherness

Marianne Vaatstra was sixteen when her body was found on a meadow in the rural area of Friesland (in the north of the Netherlands). This was on May 1, 1999, a day after the national celebration of Queen's Day. Since the crime scene was not too far away from an asylum-seekers' center, accusations were quickly directed toward "them," who happened to come from the Middle East. I will not go into the details, but this suspicion led to a lot of violence and racism vis-à-vis the inhabitants of the center and to its eventual closing.[8] The racist response to the gruesome crime grew beyond the rural area to become a national concern. In the media the asylum-seekers' center was described as "a hotbed of criminal activities."

Marianne was raped and her throat was sliced by a knife. The late right-wing politician Pim Fortuyn dedicated a column in a weekly magazine in which he labeled the manner of death as "a non-Dutch manner of killing": a remark that underlines that the suspect had to be one of "them."[9] The knife and the use of the knife became interesting racializing markers. Take, for example, the scenario that

8. See Lisette Jong and Amade M'charek, "The High-Profile Case as 'Fire Object': Following the Marianne Vaatstra Murder Case Through the Media," *Crime, Media, Culture* 14, no. 3 (2018): 347–63.

9. Pim Fortuyn, "Kollumerstront," *Elsevier* (1999). Retrieved March 14, 2021, from https://www.pimfortuyn.com/pim-fortuyn/archief-columns/165 -kollumerstront; see also Martijn De Koning, "Een Nederlander Snijdt Geen Keel Door," *Volkskrant* (2012).

the locals had in their minds. It was sketched as follows by the late Dutch crime reporter Peter R. de Vries: "The perpetrator was well prepared. Like a predator looking for a prey he was waiting to attack Marianne from the bushes. After that, he killed her by cutting her throat. Given this *modus operandus,* the suspect cannot but be an inhabitant of the asylum seekers center." This so-called *modus operandus* that was articulated by de Vries in an episode of his TV show dedicated to the Marianne Vaatstra case broadcast on May 20, 2012. To be sure, in that moment in time de Vries did not support this scenario but was merely articulating a dominant view among the local population. The scenario sketched is, one could say, a trope, as it is often encountered in the media. But to understand how it racializes, let me share another example: an excerpt from an op-ed concerning a different murder case that took place in Belgium, at Brussel central station.[10] "On video screens you can see them, like predators along the walls of the central station, waiting, alert and on the watch to find an easy prey in the passing herds of passengers for them to kill . . . The unlucky one will not stand a chance. The predators have knives. In childhood they have learned, during the annual sacrifice how to cut the throat of warm-blooded herd animals."[11] This quote helps us understand the framing of the knife, the use of knives to cut throats as well as those who tend to use knives for that purpose. Relating this to a religious custom indicates that the perpetrator is a non-Western, non-Dutch other and, more specifically, a *Muslim* man. He is inclined to violence and killing, by using a knife. Interestingly the cutting of a throat contributes to the very bestialization of the perpetrator who, through the act, becomes the Other. This Other, to draw on Deleuze and Guattari, who resists or cannot be like us becomes killable.[12] Importantly,

10. See Amade M'charek, "Silent Witness, Articulate Collective: DNA Evidence and the Inference of Visible Traits," *Bioethics* 22, no. 9 (2008): 519–28.

11. Paul Belien, *De Standaard* (2006).

12. Gilles Deleuze and Félix Guattari, *A Thousand Plateaus: Capitalism and Schizophrenia* (University of Minnesota Press, 1987).

here, is that suspicion is not directed toward any specific individual but toward a whole group: a group that is phenotypically othered through markers attributed to the assumed perpetrator, a Muslim.

This process of othering comes with a specific version of sameness. This version not only racializes; it leaves no space for differentiation within the group. All individuals are lumped together and the other way around: An individual cannot *but* stand for the whole group. This version of sameness indeed reduces a group of people to one specific quality, in this case violence. While sameness as *otherness* produces a homogeneous racialized group, in what follows we will see that sameness can also open up the category and allows for various differentiations. We will consider sameness, not related to otherness but to *us-ness*.

A Farmer from Here: On Sameness as Us-ness

Crime reporter Peter R. de Vries, whom I quoted above, had initially contributed quite a bit to suspicion vis-à-vis the asylum seekers.[13] But then a few years later, in his show of 2012, he argued that "we had it all wrong." He there revealed new clues about the case. By contrast to the scenario quoted above, Marianne was not killed by slicing her throat. She was first strangled with her bra and only then the knife was used. This, so we were told, is an indication that the perpetrator should be sought in a different population. Dedicating one edition of his TV show to the case, de Vries was actually collaborating in the criminal investigation. Over the years he had been the person most trusted by the local Frisian population, as he was adamant about seeing the case solved and kept provoking new investigations. He was therefore asked to warm up the local population in order to make them participate in a DNA dragnet in the context of familial searching. The message con-

13. See Amade M'charek et al., "The Trouble with Race in Forensic Identification," *Science, Technology, & Human Values* 45, no. 5 (2020): 804–28.

veyed was that the perpetrator was not among the participants in the dragnet, but that he might be a brother, uncle, or another male relative of the one who submitted DNA.

One month after the dragnet was completed, Peter R. de Vries tweeted: "Man arrested. White suspect. Frisian, lives 2.5 km away from crime scene. 100% DNA-match!" This tweet indicates that the perpetrator was among the participants in the dragnet, rather than a relative, for example, an uncle or a brother of one of the participants. And he was a local Frisian farmer. The response to this fact was both disturbing and arresting. It was inductive for the way sameness as us-ness figures and how it contributes to processes of racialization. A forensic investigator expressed his surprise as follows: "Jasper [the suspect] was just about the last person on whose door you would be knocking, with his farm and little family and all. Because you tend to presuppose a usual criminal." And the father of the victim pondered: "So it is someone from our midst (*van ons*), a *farmer*, a *white man*." I was indeed alerted to the production of sameness through the sense of community that emerged when the identity of the suspect was revealed. This was not a community of violence and aggression vis-à-vis the (phenotypic) other or the suspect, but a community of care vis-à-vis "us" and those who belong to "us."

It is remarkable that the suspect was addressed as a white man. In a context where whiteness is the norm, it hardly ever gets articulated. However, in this case, despite the huge investment in DNA familiar searching and by consequence, the hypothesis that the suspect was related to the local population, the whiteness of the suspect still sparked surprise and disbelief. It thus marked the persistent suspicion that was placed on migrants and refugees, a group that was phenotypically othered. But whiteness was also related to the occupation of the suspect, being a farmer who takes care of his dairy cows and someone with lots of land. The link between Frisian whiteness and his traditional occupation further alerted me to race. While any of these markers by itself does not necessarily enact race, together they become a potent technology of racialization.[14] The occupation of the suspect that we already encountered previously was something that came up again and again in the media. A fellow villager of the suspect was quoted as saying: "'Well, DNA doesn't lie,' mumbles Nycklo de Vries (19). But it remains hard to believe. He knew the arrested man. Just like everyone else, here in Oudwoude. A very normal, social man. *With a lot of land and a livestock farm.* Married, a son and daughter in her twenties."[15] In another account of what the villagers were going through, we read: "Yesterday people in Oudwoude responded with dismay to the arrest of the *friendly fellow townsman,* who was always in for a chat with everyone. His family was quickly relocated to a quiet area. *His nearly 100 dairy cows are being looked after.*"[16] To underscore his care for his livestock, the suspect declares in court that he and his father went out at eleven 'o clock to milk the cows, on the evening of the rape and murder of Marianne Vaatstra.[17] "He is one of us, a farmer from our midst," as the father of Vaatstra said. This coupling between whiteness, land, and relation to the land, as well as activity (caring for his cows) or occupation (being a farmer), is a classical way of racializing a community.[18] However, though the suspect was made a member of a community of us-ness through his color, occupation, and relation to land, the accounts above also make space for him as an individual. He is somebody everybody knows, he is kind, normal, a social man, and has a friendly word for everybody. Also, in a long and

14. The racialization of the Frisian identity has a vested history in Dutch physical anthropology; see Rob van Ginkel, "Antropologie Van Nederland," *Sociologische gids* 42, no. 1 (1995): 7–59

15. In *Trouw,* November 20, 2012 (emphasis added).

16. In *Dagblad van het Noorden,* November 20, 2012 (emphasis added).

17. See https://nos.nl/artikel/489559-jasper-s-doet-huilend-z-n-verhaal.html (last accessed July 11, 2023).

18. Other well-known examples of groups that have historically been racialized and classified through occupation are the Roma people and the Jewish people. See Mihai Surdu, *Those Who Count: Expert Practices of Roma Classification* (Central European University Press, 2016).

calm interview with his lawyer, the viewer is presented a portrait, not of a monster or beast but of a torn person, full of remorse and shame for his uncontrolled behavior on that night thirteen years before.[19] In an interview about this TV appearance, his lawyer Jan Vlug said, "There I have tried to portray Jasper as a human being, as a nice man who had done something horrible."[20] This room for individuality, I want to suggest, is a key element of this version of sameness in relation to us-ness. Where the coupling of sameness and otherness takes away all individuality and reduces individuals to a homogeneous and othered group, *sameness in relation to us-ness,* on the other hand, *makes space for individuality.* In this case the suspect-ness of the suspect came as a surprise because he was so normal and kind. More generally, this retention of individuality is key to the proverbial "rotten apple" that does not impact the identity of the whole group. This is a mechanism through which white right-wing terrorism often leads to a psychologization of the suspects (think of the Norwegian Adres Berivik), rather than the default mobilization of culture, background, or religion as typical explanations in cases of, say, Muslim terrorism.

Sameness in relation to us-ness makes room for individuality but it does more than this. Already, as seen previously, the suspect was referred to as a family man: He is married with a son and a daughter in her twenties. The family figured prominently in the care articulated by the local villagers. The municipality organized a meeting for the villagers after which the interviewed mayor was reported saying, "About 300 residents showed up in the village hall. Bilker [the mayor] speaks after a 'modest and heartwarming' meeting. The village will not let the family down, he says. The mayor knows the parents of the arrested man. 'They are overloaded with

19. See https://www.youtube.com/watch?v=HpoU5e8EuTI (last accessed July 11, 2023).

20. See Lex Meulenbroek and Paul Poley, *Kroongetuige DNA: Onzichtbaar spoor in spraakmakende zaken* (Bezige Bij bv, Uitgeverij De, 2014), 452.

cards, phone calls and best wishes expressing support. That gives a good feeling.'"[21] This excerpt makes clear that the family aspect of sameness is not only the fact that the suspect has children, but that he himself is a child of parents who are also part of the same community. The mayor of the village Oudwoude continues:

> Everyone knows the parents; they are very well known in the village. Imagine: you lead a very normal life and then suddenly something like this happens. It was my pleasure to convey the commonly shared feeling among the inhabitants of Oudwoude. The feeling of: "You belong here, you belong" (*Jullie horen hier, jullie horen erbij*). The parents were very happy with that. They responded very emotionally, in tears. They are doing reasonably well under the circumstances. . . . . I did expect that something like "we stand by and around the family" (*we staan om de familie heen*) would arise, but I am pleasantly surprised that it is so strong.[22]

It took me some time to understand how this care for the *parents* of the suspect was relevant and to see that it signals a particular family relation. Here the suspect is not merely a family man, with his own household and children. What these quotes make clear is that the suspect is addressed as a child, the child of *someone*. Thus, by caring for the parents, the suspect becomes a child. This obviously evokes a sense of "innocence"—even if the child is a man who is forty-five years old, he is still addressed as the object of care and concern for his parents.[23] In addition, the attention to the parents puts the suspect in a genealogical relation, a relation of kinship. In this way we come to realize that not only does the suspect have a family and children of his own who deserve care and attention, but he has parents, and probably grandparents, and thus a history in that place. The continuation of kinship produces a *longue durée*

21. In *Trouw*, November 21, 2012.

22. In *Dagblad van het Noorden*, November 22, 2012.

23. On the crucial and complicated politics of innocence, see Miriam Ticktin, "A World Without Innocence," *American Ethnologist* 44, no. 4 (2017): 577–90.

and a historical connection to the place, to Friesland and the village Oudwoude. "You belong *here*," said the mayor.

This brief analysis of events makes clear that here, racialization is related not only to color—whiteness—but also crucially to religion (churchgoing people), lineage (the suspect has children and is the child of someone), and belonging to a place as well as occupation (farming). Moreover, sameness as *us-ness* encompasses not only the community but also the family, as well as individuality. This rendering is in stark contrast to sameness as otherness, which is intolerant for differences within, as it makes the individual stand for the collective.

Doing Race and Sameness in "Europe's Migration Crisis"

As indicated, it was the Marianne Vaatstra case that alerted me to the issue of race and sameness. Precisely because I have been following it closely for years and have been analyzing it in so many instances it allowed me to uncage race as it were. It allowed me to pause with it and look at it with fresh eyes. Once I unraveled the way sameness as us-ness operated and how it produced a very slippery version of race, I started to see it functioning in many more cases. In what follows I want to go briefly into race and sameness through the example of what is called "Europe's refugee crisis." I will attend to two instances, one from 2015 and one from 2022.

Doing Sameness, Racializing the Migrant Other

The issue of migration and the fact that large groups of people are on the move in an attempt to find refuge constitute a wide and large problem. Yet, what has come to be known as "Europe's migration crisis" is inextricably linked to the uprisings in the Arab world. These started as democratic movements in 2011 in Tunisia, Egypt, Yemen, Libya, Bahrain, and Syria, but soon resulted in crises and massive violence in many of these countries as well as the ongoing war in Syria. These political changes led not only to political instability in countries such as Libya (one of the transit countries for migrants) but also to an increasing number of migrants and refugees who tried to reach Europe.

In the midst of the enfolding crises, the EU response has consistently focused on care, not for people in need, but for Europe's borders.[24] Casting Europe's borders as vulnerable and in need of attention has led to their ongoing expansion and militarization.[25] The lack of infrastructure and care for the people who were fleeing war (especially from Syria), and who were trying to reach Europe, had caught the attention of the masses when, in the summer of 2015 the suffering of thousands upon thousands of people became public. And it was, in particular, the image of the toddler Alan Kurdi that moved the people in Europe, and beyond. The picture of the young boy washed up on the shore of the Turkish coast town Bodrum has produced proximity to the people who were knocking on Europe's door. This child, dressed with care in a red T-shirt, blue shorts, and leather shoes, could have been your own or that of your neighbors.

Despite the powerful effect of the picture, soon the political mood would start to flip, first with the Paris Bataclan terrorist attacks in November 2015, and a month later with the sexual violence against women on New Year's Eve in German Cologne. On that evening, a large number of women were victims of robbery and sexual harassment by young men that acted in groups on the public square of Cologne where the celebrations took place. The welcoming mood in Europe started to make way for suspicion and fear vis-à-vis the other.

While these horrific events helped legitimate the restrictive and inhumane border management regimes, they also contributed to the racialization and sexualization of the other. There was, however, a

24. See Giuseppe Campesi, "The Arab Spring and the Crisis of the European Border Regime: Manufacturing Emergency in the Lampedusa Crisis," *Robert Schuman Centre for Advanced Studies Research Paper* 2011/59 (2011). http://hdl.handle.net/1814/19375

25. See Mark Akkerman, "Militarization of European Border Security," *The Emergence of EU Defense Research Policy: From Innovation to Militarization* (2018): 337–55.

remarkable difference between the initial responses to Paris and to Cologne. In the framing of the terrorist attack in Paris it was Islam and religious fundamentalism that were foregrounded. Pictures would show how innocent and calm Paris would be attacked by a Muslim sniper from an unexpected corner. The depiction of the attack in words and images portrayed the perpetrators as funda-mentalist, fanatics, enemies of democracy, modernity, and civiliza-tion. By contrast, in the Cologne events the perpetrators were not Muslim fanatics per se. They were, after all, drinking and partying, just like many others were doing on New Years' Eve. The framing in the Cologne case was rather that of the sexualized Arab, who poses a threat to "our" women and to "our" modern ways of living.[26]

Although references to the "refugee crisis" were implied in the responses to the Paris attacks, in Cologne they were made explicit. For example, Cologne's chief police, Wolfgang Albers, stated that "the overwhelming majority" of suspects were asylum seekers and illegal immigrants who had recently arrived in Germany, and he went on to suggest that they were men of "Arab or North African appearance." Importantly, there were hardly any pictures of the events is Cologne. The images available showed a crowd of people on the square between the central station and the Cologne Cathedral lighting fireworks. Perhaps the very lack of pictures captured the public's imaginary. It led to various representations, which seem-ingly attempted to both capture and transform the issue.

I will highlight two examples that were published in well-respected German and Dutch newspapers. One illustration in the German *Süddeutschen Zeitung* accompanied an article called "Auf Armlänge" (At arm's length); a denunciatory reference to a state-ment made the mayor of Cologne, Henriette Reker, in which her primary response was to advise victims of sexual violence to keep these men at an arm's length.[27] The graphic black-and-white im-

26. See Beverly Weber, "The German Refugee 'Crisis' After Cologne: The Race of Refugee Rights," *English Language Notes* 54, no. 2 (2016): 77–92.
27. *Süddeutsche Zeitung,* January 9/10, 2016.

age clearly shows a black arm groping a white woman between the legs. The impression of a threatening Black sexuality, a sexuality that is invading (our?) white women, cannot be misunderstood. The Dutch newspapers chose an oriental depiction for one of its cover pages, from a painting by Otto Pilny, from 1910, called "The Slave Market Presentation," to accompany an extended op-ed in which the Arab man was depicted as backward, with an animal-like sexuality, and therefore not ready to deal with emancipated and independent white women.[28] In the image we find ourselves in a desert with a caravan in the back as well as a Bedouin tent. Central in the painting are two delighted Arab men each holding an enslaved woman, one of them completely naked and white, displaying them to invisible buyers. The idea conveyed by the image was of an Arabic man for whom the white woman is both a commodity and an object of sexual desire. In these examples and the debates that ensued, migrants were not per se discussed as people who hate our democracy, or civilization, but as people who never arrived in modernity—as if still in a state of nature, caught up in their sexual drives. Sexuality thus became a hinge to casting the refugees as a threat and to racialize them. On January 13, 2016, the French *Charlie Hebdo* published a cartoon that underscored the racialization through sexualization in a blunt way. In the upper left corner, we see a small image, a reminder of the toddler's body on the beach. The main image shows two adult men chasing after two panicking women. The main text reads: "what would little Aylan have become if he had grown up?" The answer is given at the bottom of the cartoon. "A buttocks scooter in Germany."

One could say that the sexualization of the migrant other makes the threat even more visceral, than a representation of the migrant as a terrorist. The potentiality of his proximity and the violation not of our democracy but of our body feeds into the racist sentiments that have surfaced since these events. The *Charlie Hebdo*

28. *NRC*, January 9/10, 2016.

cartoon points in a radical way to a version of sameness, namely sameness as otherness. There are no "innocent migrants," if that's what the image of Alan Kurdi is trying to show. All migrants and refugees are bound to turn into this sexual threat, invading our (white European) bodies. This version of sameness, then, racializes through sexualization,[29] where the threat of proximity necessarily provokes a response, namely that of distance, exclusion and ultimately, expulsion.

During the past year these sentiments vis-à-vis refugees had flipped dramatically in Europe. Let us take a loop from 2015/16 to 2022 and consider how next to sameness as otherness a sameness as us-ness emerged.

Doing Sameness, Racializing Europe

While the problems of migration and EU responses have accumulated and have become ever uglier, with thousands upon thousands of deaths at Europe's borders, and while Poland was building walls that trapped migrants and refugees who were trying to find refuge, in February 2022 the war in the Ukraine began. Within the first seven days, almost two million people fled from Ukraine and found a welcoming Europe.[30] Governments, the public, and the private sector responded generously, helping people find shelter. Although all those who need shelter should be offered such, it was surprising, as many have observed, to see the difference in sentiment and response toward the refugees from Ukraine versus those from Syria, for example. For my proposes here, the discourse of sameness, and the sense of community and belonging is striking and interesting.

---

29. The classic here is Frantz Fanon, *Black Skin, White Masks* (Grove/Atlantic, 2008 [1967]).

30. See *UNIICR (2022) Private Sector Donates over US$200 Million to UNHCR's Ukraine Emergency Response*. Available from https://www.unhcr.org/news/news-releases/private-sector-donates-over-us200-million-unhcrs-ukraine-emergency-response.

To be clear, the problem of Ukrainian refugees and borders is way too complex to address in this chapter.[31] Here, I will limit myself to a small collection of quotes from the media to tease out everyday and almost innocent markers that together produce a racialized version of sameness.[32]

Propagating a politics of xenophobia and expulsion, and while building a wall to keep other people out, Poland opened its arms to welcome hundreds of thousands of refugees from Ukraine, as did other neighboring countries. To explain this political shift in sentiment, in a conversation with journalists, the Bulgarian prime minister Kiril Petkov was quoted as saying: "These are not the refugees we are used to . . . these people are *Europeans* . . . . These people are *intelligent,* they are *educated* people . . . . This is not the refugee wave we have been used to, people we were not sure about their identity, people with unclear pasts, who could have been even terrorists."[33] The Ukrainian Deputy Chief Prosecutor, David Sakvarelidze, was interviewed on *BBC* saying, "It's very emotional for me because I see *European people with blue eyes and blonde hair being killed.*"[34]

Various journalists were trying to make sense of the welcoming mode they were witnessing. On NBC, journalist Kelly Cobiella commented on this difference as follows: "Just to put it bluntly, these are not refugees from Syria, these are refugees from neighbor-

31. See, Nina Rosstalnyj, *Deserving and Undeserving Refugees? An Analysis of the EU's Response to the 'Refugee Crisis' in 2015 Compared to the Refugee Influx from Ukraine in 2022* (Master's thesis, Central European University), https://www.etd.ceu.edu/2022/rosstalnyj_nina.htm, 2022.

32. See Reinhard A. Weisser, "A Near-Real-Time Analysis of Societal Responses to Ukrainian Refugee Migration in Europe," *International Migration* (2022).

33. Anthony Faiola et al., "Suddenly Welcoming, Europe Opens the Door to Refugees Fleeing Ukraine," March 1, 2022, https://www.washingtonpost.com/world/2022/02/28/ukraine-refugees-europe/.

34. "'European People with Blue Eyes and Blonde Hair Being Killed' What a BBC Interviewee Commented," February 28, 2022, https://www.youtube.com/watch?v=pU-8gKaUO_Y.

ing Ukraine. That, quite frankly, is part of it. These are *Christians,* they're *white,* they're very *similar* people." In a similar vein, the *Al Jazeera* English reporter Peter Dobbie stated: "What's compelling is looking at them, the way they are *dressed.* These are prosperous, middle-class people. These are not obviously refugees trying to get away from the Middle East . . . or North Africa. *They look like any European family that you'd live next door to.*"[35] And Daniel Hannan (*The Daily Telegraph*) commented: "They *seem so like us.* That is what makes it so shocking. Ukraine is a European country. Its people *watch Netflix* and have *Instagram* accounts, vote in free elections and read uncensored newspapers."[36]

It is clear that these refugees are different from other refugees, refugees from Syria, for example. These refugees are part of "us." Just like we saw through the forensic case, sameness as us-ness makes space for individuality, family, and belonging to a community. And just like in that case, religion (Christianity) and whiteness are mobilized as markers of racial belonging. But what is striking are the variety and details of everyday markers of us-ness that have been mobilized to produce sameness and to make them part of us-ness. Blue eyes, blond hair, whiteness, Christianity, well dressed, intelligent, Netflix watching, using Instagram—all become markers of making us-ness: all become markers for making race. Importantly here is that what is racialized, through these very details, is not just Ukrainian refugees but Europe itself. Europe, as democratic, Christian, white, and modern, emerges as the space and a community to which Ukraine, as families and individuals, belong and to which they contribute.

35. Moustafa Bayoumi, "They Are 'Civilised' and 'Look like Us': The Racist Coverage of Ukraine," March 2, 2022, https://www.theguardian.com/commentisfree/2022/mar/02/civilised-european-look-like-us-racist-coverage-ukraine.

36. Daniel Hannan, "Vladimir Putin's Monstrous Invasion Is an Attack on Civilisation Itself," February 26, 2022, https://www.telegraph.co.uk/news/2022/02/26/vladimir-putins-monstrous-invasion-attack-civilisation/.

Conclusion

I opened this chapter with an invitation to become more curious about race. Race can perhaps be likened to the Greek mythical figure of the Hydra: a gigantic water-snake-like monster with nine heads, of which one is immortal. While both virulent and ubiquitous, race also tends to be a surprise, so that we cannot assume we know it beforehand. What if we were to uncage race and go beyond default answers as to what it is, I suggested. Inspired by Foucault on the potentials of curiosity, I have elaborated one avenue for an open-ended inquisitiveness about what race is and explored a mode of care as to how we might study it. By shifting perspective on race, from a matter that pivots around difference to one that could be also studied through the lens of sameness, my aim was twofold: to articulate different modes of racialization, and to learn what race is made to be in practice.

In order to attend to sameness, I suggested the need to distinguish between sameness as otherness and sameness as us-ness. I then elaborated how the racialization of otherness tends to lump people together to become those others who are excludable, while the racialization of us-ness is tolerant for differences within and is geared toward making people belong to us. The practices of racialization and modes of doing sameness indeed contribute to different versions of the biohuman, those who belong here and those who should be expelled or kept at bay.

The biohuman is inherently a nature-culture assemblage. Paying close attention to how groups of people get racialized, we saw how not only processes of naturalization and biologization but also mundane objects come to play a role. We have seen how a knife comes to racialize Muslims, making them other; how caring for your cattle contributes to Dutch whiteness; how watching Netflix helps make Ukrainians fit into a naturalized white European category. In practice these unassuming markers of difference, markers that seem indifferent to race, can become crucial, precisely because race is not a singular thing. It is never simply biology or simply a cultural feature. Rather, race is a fluid assemblage in which a variety of cultural markers and features of the body are always part of the equation. Race as a key component of the biohuman will always have an element of surprise and thus urges us to remain open and curious about it.

3. Caging, Staging: Race and the Question of Human Life in Covid Times

Nadine Ehlers

AT 7:00 A.M. ON JULY 9, 2021, horse-mounted officers and hundreds of other police personnel descended into racial-minority communities in Southwestern Sydney with the purported aim of combating the spread of the Delta variant of Covid-19. This "special operation" also deployed traffic and highway patrol officers, dog units, and police surveillance helicopters in the geospatial region the *Sydney Morning Herald* reported was "ground zero" for Delta.[1] In another article, the newspaper relayed that this operation marked "an escalation of the state's public health order enforcement, [and that] senior [police] officers said the high-visibility effort . . . was needed because breaches were persisting despite ongoing community engagement to inform people of their responsibilities."[2] Police

---

1. See "Sydney's South-West Now Ground Zero for Covid," *The Sydney Morning Herald,* July 8, 2021, https://www.smh.com.au/national/sydney-s-south-west-now-ground-zero-for-covid-19-outbreak-20210708-p5883n.html.
2. Hunter Fergus, "Show of Force: How NSW Police Took Command to Combat COVID-19," *The Sydney Morning Herald,* November 28, 2020, https://www.smh.com.au/national/nsw/show-of-force-how-nsw-police-took-command-to-combat-covid-19-20201126-p56i7s.html.

were out in droves in these targeted areas, cordoning them off and essentially corralling the inhabitants through strict quarantine. While wider Sydney was eventually placed under a 107-day hard lockdown, no other parts of Sydney had comparable restrictions or modalities of visible policing imposed. As one politician noted, "there is absolutely no logic for the direct targeting of Sydney's black and brown communities. . . . The *only* logic for targeting the most multicultural part of Sydney is the racist over policing of people of colour."[3]

This chapter takes a critical biohumanities approach to explore the racialized biosecuritization of health in Covid times in Sydney: that is, the racialized logics and practices of the biosecurity calculus and apparatus. Specifically, I examine how the idea of the human contoured biological and social life along lines of race via two key quarantine technologies deployed in the Sydney case. The first technology was a regulatory and disciplinary taming—a *caging* (or carceral control), which was applied in distinct and disparate ways across the population, such that certain subjects were rendered lesser "human," in line with the human/animal binary opposition of Western liberalism. The second technology was spectacle—a particular *staging* (or exhibition) of minority spaces and residents, highlighting how race functions as an ontological caesura within the infrastructure of the state. I want to suggest that together these technologies could be seen as in part informed by a zoological perspective, and to constitute what we might call "zoological governance"—a form of governing relating to or affecting "lower animals." Such governance does not exclude or expel minoritized/racialized subjects from the general populace. Instead, it pursues a form of *conditional incorporation* to maintain racial reasoning and racial order.

---

3. See "Police COVID Crackdown in South-West Sydney Slammed as Racist and Heavy-handed," *The New Daily,* July 9, 2021, https://thenewdaily .com.au/news/2021/07/09/coronavirus-police-sydney/.

Racialized Regimes of the Human and the Carceral Milieu

Faced with the biosecurity threat of Covid-19, nations around the world labored to securitize their populations through the generalized carceral milieu of quarantine, lockdown, and isolation. Like many nation-states, Australia instituted quarantine measures that restricted individuals' movements by way of health policy mandates, heightened visibility (to make sure individuals and communities followed those mandates), and efforts to have individuals internalize governance of the self—against infection. The surveillance of space and individuals within it was key here. Tracking cases and morbidity, tracing contact vector points, testing blackwater/sewage, maintaining border controls, and requiring and reporting on population screening/testing (alongside genomic sequencing) were the most common forms of surveillance adopted to minimize the spread of the virus under conditions of quarantine. Given that quarantine was concerned with the protection and promotion of human life—"making life live"—it can be viewed as a care practice. Importantly, however, it can also cause harm, precisely because it can involve gradations of carcerality and distinct forms of biosecuritization based on gradations of the "human."

To begin making sense of this claim, it is first necessary to consider the conceptual category of the "human" as that which is *produced* rather than natural or ontologically self-evident. Despite the fact that "we" are animals too, taxonomical borders have been erected between what we name as the "human" and the "animal," with each positioned as putatively discreet categories. Indeed, the animal has been cast as the opposable limit to the figure of the human. Human and animal have been rendered separate because the human has been understood as being able to *transcend their basic biological animality*, to rise above their status as living animal. Human exceptionalism—that which makes "us" supposedly distinct from nonhuman animals—is to be found, so the logic goes, in the human capacity for reason, rationality, agency, knowledge production, and culture, and humans supposedly *humanize* themselves through a *repudiation of animality* so as to assume the form of the "cultural moral" human.[4] As many animal studies scholars and others have established, these logics produce a discourse of speciesism, whereby humans are considered more morally important in species differentiation, species are differentially treated based on species membership, and nonhuman animals are excluded from the protections granted to humans.

As others have demonstrated, however, the invention of the human as an ontological category was always accompanied by the entwined production of "marginalized non/personhood," highlighting that the discourse of species difference has been put to other uses: It is *not only* applied to nonhuman animals.[5] The discourse of species "will always be available for use by some humans against other humans . . . to countenance violence against the other of *whatever* species—or gender, or race, or class, or sexual difference."[6] Certain peoples have long been viewed as occupying lower positions in the Enlightenment ladder of civilizations, with "elite" white humans taken as "truly human" and distinguished from "lower" life forms, including nonhuman animals, working-class people, and people of color. Those designated outside the boundaries of whiteness have been understood as deficient in reason, higher feeling, and self-control, and they have been positioned as driven by impulse, as more aligned with the body and with nature. As such, racialized subjects have often been cast as "wild" and in need of taming, a reality Frantz Fanon marked when discussing the process of colonization. As he

4. As Foucault famously argues, "for millennia, man remained what he was for Aristotle: a living animal with the additional capacity for a political existence." Michel Foucault, *The History of Sexuality Volume 1: The Will to Knowledge* (Penguin Books, 1998), 176.

5. See, for instance, Zakiyah Iman Jackson, *Becoming Human: Matter and Meaning in an Antiblack World* (Duke University Press, 2020). Also see Megan Glick, *Infrahumanisms: Science, Culture, and the Making of Modern Non/personhood* (Duke University Press, 2018).

6. Cary Wolfe, *Animal Rites: American Culture, the Discourse of Species, and Posthumanist Theory* (University of Chicago Press, 2003), 8.

observed, "discipline, tame, subdue, and now pacify are the common terms used by the colonialists in the territories occupied."[7] The discourse of species has enabled "Western civilizations" to define themselves against those populations deemed *insufficiently human* or "dubiously human."[8]

In the extreme, this discourse has also enabled what Cary Wolfe calls a "moral economy" whereby certain humans can be killed "by marking *them* as animal."[9] In Frantz Fanon's *Wretched of the Earth,* the animality in question is that of the colonized or the native, Black and otherwise. As he states: "In plain talk, he is reduced to the state of an animal. And consequently, when the colonizer speaks of the colonized he uses zoological terms. Allusion is made to the slithery movements of the yellow race, the odors from the 'native' quarters, to the hordes, the stink, the swarming, the seething and the gesticulations. In his endeavors of description and finding the right word, the colonist refers constantly to the bestiary."[10] Such ideas were generated from the earliest days of modern racial thought—which adapted classical and medieval beliefs in *scala naturæ* or the Great Chain of Being, a hierarchical system that ranked all creation and saw humans as sharing an affinity with animals, with the "lowest" human beings viewed as closest to the "highest" animals—and reached their crescendo in late eugenic logics and practices. This is not to say, however, that the idea of the insufficiently human has disappeared.

Gradations of the human persist in the ongoing biopolitical governance of the population and the promotion of its welfare, where certain humans have clearly counted more in terms of lives to be fostered. Such governance operates through scientific understandings

7. Frantz Fanon, *The Wretched of the Earth,* trans. Richard Philcox (Grove Press, 2004), 228.

8. Judith Butler, *Precarious Life: The Powers of Mourning and Violence* (Verso, 2006), 91.

9. Wolfe, *Animal Rites,* 6.

10. Fanon, *Wretched of the Earth,* 7.

of the *biological properties of the human as species:* it serves, as David Chandler and Julian Reid have argued, "to reduce the life of the human to its biological capacities, conceiving the human in the form of 'the biohuman.'"[11] If biopolitics protects "biohumanity"/human biological life in its generality, those deemed insufficiently human are not only devalued but are often seen to be a *threat* to biohumanity. And, as Michel Foucault insists, where biopolitics adjudicates species life—to "subdivide the species it controls"—it *justifies exposing to death* ("letting die" or, in the extreme, killing) those citizens who are viewed as a threat,[12] supposedly to protect biohumanity—the broader population who are preferentially valued.

During the Delta outbreak in Sydney, particular non-white communities were positioned as a health and biosecurity risk/threat, to be addressed by management and control in a way that suggests they were viewed as insufficiently human. The claim here is not that racialized minorities were depicted as animals: This would be too simplistic a read. Rather, the power/knowledge relation or discourse of species *conditioned the biopolitical administration of life* during the Sydney Covid-19 Delta outbreak in ways we might call *zoological.* If the subdivision of (human) species is central to the biopolitical administration of life, efforts to manage and control those viewed as insufficiently human—within the broader operation of biopolitics—constitute what could be referred to as "zoological governance."

Zoological governance is *predicated on the logic that certain beings are "lesser" (animals),* as determined by the discourse of species difference, and more aligned with untamed bodily nature. It *manages the social sphere according to this logic,* via technologies often

11. David Chandler and Julian Reid, *The Neoliberal Subject: Resilience, Adaptation and Vulnerability* (Rowman and Littlefield International, 2016), 108.

12. Michel Foucault, *Society Must Be Defended: Lectures at the Collège de France 1975–1976,* ed. Mauro Bertani and Alessandro Fontana, trans. David Macey (Picador, 2003), 255.

reserved for the collection, keeping, and exhibition of nonhuman animals and those historically situated in the liminal space between human and animal. This management confirms and augments the supposed lesser status of these peoples, perversely justifying operations of "let die." In what follows, I trace out two key technologies deployed in the operations of zoological governance in the Sydney case: carcerality/caging and spectacle/staging. Carcerality is the primary mode of power in modern societies, where surveillance and discipline are diffused as principals of social organization.[13] What makes this case specific is that rather than being based on inclusion with the aim of normalization, carcerality here seemingly dehumanizes and excludes those marked as racial others (ideas I later trouble). And, while spectacle supposedly disappears in carceral society, we see here that in the management of racial others it remains a key mode of power. Zoological governance, needless to say, generated unequal harms and led to dire consequences for the health of those in these communities and health equity more broadly.

Fence-in, Immobilize, Tame

The noun *cage* evokes notions of a structure of bars or wires in which birds or other animals are kept, or a prison cell or camp. The verb *caged* denotes confinement, constraint, or enclosure. In the broadest sense, it is possible to think of *race* as caged within the constraints of dominant epistemologies that delimit what race can *be* and *mean*. But we can also consider race itself as a caging mechanism that ensnares and restricts—in differential fashion—all those it marks under its terms. Caging, as it relates to race, is not simply metaphoric or discursive but instead has what Foucault called an "awesome materiality":[14] it institutes tangible, material

---

13. Michel Foucault, *Discipline and Punish: The Birth of the Prison,* trans. Alan Sheridan (Penguin, 1991).

14. Michel Foucault, "The Discourse on Language," in *The Archaeology of Knowledge* (Pantheon, 1972), 216.

effects, primarily that of (again) producing bodies—the flesh of the other—that need to be put in place. It is a *material technology* that, following philosopher Charles Mills, demarcates "civil" from "wild" spaces—and those who reside in them.[15]

In Sydney, this racialized and racializing technology of regulatory caging (or carceral control) was deployed almost a year into the pandemic, when the Delta outbreak hit in mid-June 2021. Delta initially appeared in the predominantly white and affluent Eastern suburbs, and moved through the city until June 26, when a citywide hard lockdown was put in place via an amendment to the state's *Public Health Act 2010* (NSW): strict stay-at-home orders were issued, and all essential businesses and schools closed. Such measures were adopted to secure life: biohumanity at large. However, what unfolded became a tale of two cities, where certain subjects were marked as distinct and efforts to affirm life actually exposed racial minorities to deadly conditions.[16]

This particular part of the story began a few weeks into the general lockdown, when three regions in the city's Southwest were identified as hot spot "areas of concern"—later expanding to twelve areas throughout the Southwest and West. These areas, with high migrant, Black, brown, Asian, and refugee populations, were placed under restrictions never introduced in the East. Though there had been clusters of infection across the city prior to this, authorities justified the imposition of harsher restrictions in these areas because transmission case rates were rising rapidly in the Southwest, home to "essential workers" who were unable to shelter in place. Increasing infection rates were blamed on residents of these areas who officials repeatedly claimed were *flouting* Covid safety rules: not wearing masks or wearing them incorrectly, engaging in unnecessary travel, gathering in large groups, and living in extended or intergenerational family homes (a marker of racial otherness).

---

15. Charles Mills, *The Racial Contract* (Cornell University Press, 1997), 41.
16. On this concept see Nadine Ehlers and Shiloh Krupar, *Deadly Biocultures: The Ethics of Life-Making* (University of Minnesota Press, 2019).

What subsequently emerged was a *spatialization of preemption*—to "stop the spread"—*achieved through a distinct form of carcerality.*

These areas were demarcated as internal spaces (within the broader city) to be contained and made subject to spatially specific control, surveillance, and policing, precisely because the bodies and behaviors of those residing within these spaces were deemed to be "problematic." The racialization of these communities (and evocation of the discourse of species) became clear when the state health minister said that "people from other backgrounds . . . don't seem to think that it is necessary to comply with the law and . . . don't really give great consideration to what they do in terms of its impact on the rest of the community . . . [I] say to them, you need to because otherwise the forces of the law are coming after you."[17] With this statement, "people from other backgrounds" (that is, non-white) were named as distinct and cast as uncontrolled, and the response suggests they needed subdual or taming.

The first method of caging these populations was via confinement—marking the parameters of the cage and enclosing and isolating those within this internal "wildspace" who supposedly did not "comply with the law." This was achieved through the specific public health measure of "ring-fencing."[18] As a term, *ring-fencing* is used in finance to distinguish between assets and liabilities; in politics it marks the history of the 1970s Belfast police strategy (later adopted in London) of erecting fences around major vehicle access points to halt the movements of the IRA—in this incarnation it refers to defending against terrorists; in farming, the term is used to demarcate farmland, mainly to enclose domesticated animals.

17. Rashida Yosufzai and Janice Petersen, "Gladys Berejiklian Defends Brad Hazzard Over 'Other Backgrounds' Comment," *SBSNews,* September 16, 2021, https://www.sbs.com.au/news/article/gladys -berejiklian-defends-brad-hazzard-over-other-backgrounds-comment /0vt3pgrhm.

18. The New South Wales state government did not officially adopt "ring-fencing," but the restrictions and lockdown of particular regions amounted to ring-fencing, even if it was not named as such.

In public health, to ring-fence is to identify and isolate hot spots of infection. While this strategy was applied in Australia at multiple scales—to control the borders of the nation and borders between various states—the harshest form of ring-fencing was applied to these minority hot spots. Here, the specter of liabilities, terrorism (from the Latin root, *terror:* the use of extreme fear to intimidate people), and domestication converged in ring-fencing *within* the parameters of city.

These areas were represented again and again in the media through visual maps that marked the fencing operation—often in bright danger red, while the rest of city was shown to recede in an unmarked blur (a point I return to in the following section). The mass inside these areas were targeted and homogenized as the threatening other, lacking the fundamental attributes that supposedly distinguish the modern human. For instance, broader (whiter, richer) Sydney was called on to use "common sense" in relation to the generalized health restrictions announced in the daily press conferences from the state premier and other authorities, essentially leaving them to interpret mandates as they pleased. The fact that these new emerging hot spots required extra-constraining measures suggests those residents were somehow culturally deficient, with compromised capacity for reason and control. The idea that these people represented a threat to securitizing public health was made clear when the state premier claimed that "the risk of seeding in other parts of the city remains . . . we [need to] have a high level of vigilance, particularly for those areas that border the suburbs that we're most concerned about."[19] What became evident as this process unfolded was that these zones of carcerality were *simultaneously geographies of* securitization *and* abandonment. The stated aim

19. Emily Cosenza, "Suburbs of 'Great Concern' to Health Authorities as NSW Outbreak Grows," *The Australian,* August 23, 2021, https://www.theaustralian.com.au/breaking-news/suburbs-of-great -concern-to-health-authorities-as-nsw-outbreak-grows/news-story /99152f6e1567a625dfb93e24e7410035.

was to protect society at large, *including* those within these areas, but the isolation of this cage began to look a lot like protecting the safety of those outside *against* (and at the expense of) those within.

With Delta on the loose, the state premier placed the police commissioner in charge of the state's response to Covid-19, appointing him to the position of "emergency operations controller." At this point, a policing rather than health approach was instituted. Unprecedented public health orders were decreed by police authority to govern those within the hot spots, with the stated aim of minimizing viral contact. Residents within "areas of concern" were prohibited from moving five kilometers from their homes, while broader Sydney could move ten kilometers. Only one person could leave the house once a day for essential goods. Only "authorized workers" in this zone of carcerality were permitted to work but were required to have a permit and mandatory Covid testing every seventy-two hours. Residents were restricted to one hour of exercise per day, while those outside these areas had no time limit. Added to this, residents had to carry proof of identification if they left home, and no one from outside these areas was allowed in, except authorized workers with a permit. Last, a 9:00 p.m. to 5:00 a.m. curfew was decreed, on policing (not health) advice, making movement between these times illegal.[20]

Extra-surveillance was also instituted to enforce the new rules in these areas—to monitor the borderlines and internal spaces of this cage. A significantly increased police presence was put on the streets to patrol both on horseback and on foot for "infringements" by those repeatedly cited as posing an enhanced risk to controlling the virus. In a most controversial move, the Australian Armed Forces were called in for lockdown "compliance enforcement," amounting to what many characterized as a "militarized army of lockdown

20. Kevin Nguyen, "Sydney Lockdown Extended for One Month as NSW Records 644 COVID-19 Cases, Four Deaths," *ABC News,* August 20, 2021, https://www.abc.net.au/news/2021-08-20/nsw-records-644-covid-19 -cases-and-four-deaths/100392702.

and occupation."[21] The police and army conducted random daily door-to-door checks to make sure residents were at home, there were road-checks on drivers, and helicopters circled over the areas, using loudspeakers to order people to stay home. Under these forms of direct targeting, residents of these communities received more than double the number of arrests and fines (compared to other regions), and they were disproportionately subjected to additional searches during "Covid stop" incidents, in what amounted to a dragnet of broader racialized profiling.[22] That these securitization measures signaled a simultaneous abandonment, as noted earlier, was captured by the mayor of one of these areas, when he stated, "This is the poorest community. . . . [Lockdown now means] [t]hey cannot afford to pay their mortgage, their rent, their bills, or put food on the table to feed their children."[23] As another commentator made clear: "It's a recurring theme that our communities are not prioritized and that we are treated as lesser."[24]

Those within this cage might be said, then, to have been *domesticated* via domination. The cage marked the periphery of unequal

21. Clifford Stott et al., "A Turning Point, Securitization, and Policing in the Context of Covid-19: Building a New Social Contract Between State and Nation?" *Policing: A Journal of Policy and Practice* 14, no. 3 (2020): 574–78, 577.

22. Anton Nilsson, "NSW Police Covid-19 Fines: Double the Amount Issued in Western Sydney Compared to Eastern Suburbs," news.com.au, August 1, 2021, https://www.news.com.au/national /nsw-act/crime/nsw-police-covid19-fines-double-the-amount-issued -in-western-sydney-compared-to-eastern-suburbs/news-story /e505c427317003d5ec5e371cf02c9a20.

23. Elias Visontay and Josh Taylor, "Tougher Covid Restrictions for Western Sydney Criticised for Threatening Wellbeing of State's Poorest," *The Guardian,* August 21, 2021, https://www.theguardian.com/australia -news/2021/aug/20/tougher-covid-restrictions-for-western-sydney -criticised-for-threatening-wellbeing-of-states-poorest.

24. Khanh Tran, "'Our Communities Are Treated as Lesser': The View from South-West Sydney's Lockdown," *Honi Soit,* July 28, 2021, https:// honisoit.com/2021/07/our-communities-are-treated-as-less-the-view-from -south-west-sydneys-lockdown/.

cultural status and mobility between those outside and those within. Those within were immobilized and effectively reduced to the status of "living animal" with the usual humanizing traits denied and human "protections" withdrawn (for instance, self-determination, protection against the deprivation of life). Like all cages, however, this was not a closed but porous system, allowing certain members of the community to move beyond the periphery for essential work. PCR testing enabled those authorized workers—in the manufacturing, food processing, care, and warehousing industries—to be temporarily individualized (in distinction to the homogenized group within the cage) in order to facilitate the needs, indeed the humanizing of others. But this was only another system of entrapment— entrapment another way: If they were already exposed to deadly conditions inside—marking a certain expendability or "killability" of these "sub-populations"—then going outside to improve their capacities for life only intensified the state of precarity. By working outside (leaving home) in jobs that keep the city functioning, their exposure to Covid was heightened, the virus spread, and these communities saw excess infection and mortality rates.

Stage, Display, Spectacularize

If caging was fundamental to the racialized zoological governance of Covid-19 in the Sydney case, the technology of visual spectacle— staging—was equally important. Etymologically, the word *spectacle* derives from the Latin root *spectare,* "to view, watch," and *specere,* "to look at." The *Oxford English Dictionary* provides a more complex set of understandings: "1. a) A specially prepared or arranged display of a more or less public nature (esp. on a large scale), forming an impressive or interesting show or entertainment for those viewing it. . . . 2. A person or thing exhibited to, or set before, the public gaze as an object either (a) of curiosity or contempt, or (b) of marvel or admiration. . . . 3. An event of striking or unusual character . . . 4. a. A sight, show, or exhibition of a specified character or description." Prepared or arranged display, more or less public, and set before the public gaze are key elements to spectacle that I want to highlight here, but also the notion of heightened attraction that is produced for those viewing a spectacle.

While spectacle has been variously theorized, I am working in line with Jonathan Crary's claim that spectacle must be understood as an "architecture of power" that creates and maintains social inequality.[25] Spectacle arranges ways of seeing (in this case, the racialized other as distinct, knowable, and lesser human) and creates both ideological and material divisions. In relation to the Sydney case, I am principally concerned with spectacles of difference, wherein racial alterity (non-whiteness) is *produced* and *resecured.*[26] Racial alterity is indeed *generated* through a regime of representation: that is, a persistent and recursive visual repertoire or racial scripting (within dominant culture) that presents bodies, identities, and communities in terms of narrow and essentialized/ naturalized characteristics. Such spectacles generally confirm and compound the discourse of species difference.

The exhibition of minority hot spots and residents within them via spectacles of racial alterity occurred in the first instance through the very *operation of geo-mapping hot spots.* Earlier, I noted one particular form of map—circulated again and again with slight variations as new hot spots emerged—which demarcated minority areas in highly visible "danger red" while other, whiter, areas of the city remained unmarked in a visual blur, thus receding in consciousness as threatening viral spaces. Another form of map showed Sydney divided by local government areas (LGAs), with sequential darkening pigmentation of areas (white and yellow, through to red and

25. Jonathan Crary, *Suspensions of Perception: Attention, Spectacle, and Modern Culture* (MIT Press, 2000).

26. See Stuart Hall, "The Spectacle of the 'Other,'" in *Representation: Cultural Representations and Signifying Practices*, ed. Stuart Hall (Sage Press, 1997).

finally black) in line with the perceived march of Covid caseloads.[27] Two key factors become evident through this map.

First, in this blackening of certain minority areas as geographies of concentrated contagion, we see that geo-mapping and its visualization *fixes the virus in place* as a spatial ontology, as if it is to be found there, essential to there, rather than mobile.[28] Moreover, this kind of visualization fails to account for conditions that give rise to increased rates of infection: that is, lack of access to health resources (such as health care or adequate culturally and linguistically specific health information), increased pre-existing conditions, lower economic status, more crowded living conditions, and so on. Health in general, and how the virus tracked across communities, needs to be understood as not simply biological or of the body but as social. Also, as Jenna Loyd reminds us, "health inequalities can be understood as spatial inequalities to the degree that health is shaped by uneven social relations and material environments. This makes the geographic scales at which people understand 'health' and 'health promotion' prime areas of conflict."[29]

Second, we also see that certain spaces, occupied by certain people, were set before the public gaze as distinct from the rest of the population. But communities were racialized and race was spectacularized here *without naming race*—in what amounted to a visual semiotics of purity/impurity, safety/danger. This ostensibly race-blind representation was accompanied by race-blind language, where de-racialized nomenclature—"area of concern," "hot spot," "people from other backgrounds"—stands in for racial otherness. Importantly, the very use of color-coding on the map,

27. See Shiloh Krupar and Nadine Ehlers, "The Racial Spectacular: Pandemic Governance Through Dashboards and State Biosecurity," *Science, Technology, and Human Values (STHV)* 0, no. 0 https://doi.org/10.1177/01622439241265641.

28. Krupar and Ehlers, "The Racial Spectacular."

29. Jenna Loyd, *Health Rights Are Civil Rights: Peace and Justice Activism in Los Angeles, 1963–1978* (University of Minnesota Press, 2014), 16.

as it is overlaid with preexisting knowledge about the racialized makeup of these spaces, predisposes the viewer to read the map in particularly racialized ways. And then this map and others like it were endlessly shown in spectacular fashion, reproducing these associations over and over again. Such maps position racialized minorities as simultaneously within and beyond (other to) the nation—*foreign to* public health governance. They are within the nation because they appear on the map, but they are outside because of color/ing, perhaps an incantation of the dark continent within. Like those on that other dark continent, these peoples are topologically represented as far away (as humans) but close *simultaneously* (because they are threatening), highlighting the interplay of proximity and distance/likeness and otherness. Ultimately, the map is a way of arranging knowledge about certain spaces and the people within them, it is a way of comprehending and relaying knowledge about viral outbreak, and it shapes the attention of and instructs the populace to view both peoples and how the virus works in particular ways.

Spectacles of racial alterity also occurred through *media coverage of residents under conditions of caging*. Here, supposed disparities or differences were *made into* spectacle, and various tropes were deployed to *produce* "lesser humans." Such operations recursively recall the living "ethnic" exhibitions of human zoos, a Western phenomenon harking from the early nineteenth century. There were various exhibitionary contexts for these human zoos: world's fairs, theaters, circuses, and public zoological gardens. But the underlying logic regardless of context was to *show* the lesser varieties or typologies of humans (and the lesser or indeed inhuman behaviors naturalized to them) within an overarching system that presumed hierarchization led by white Europeans. Spectacle here was an operation of power that simultaneously marked and produced gradations of humans. If, as Lisa Uddin argues, traditional zoos and their species display endorsed the idealized human subject/spectator as racialized white—"through immersion in its own fantasy of autonomy, reason, benevolence, morality, mobility, and invisibility"[30]—human zoos only compounded this operation. Especially after the 1859 publication of Charles Darwin's *Origin of the Species* (and the subsequent rise of the discourse of evolution), the "ethnic peoples" in these displays "became easily defined as 'missing links' between human and other animal forms on an increasingly fluid chain of being."[31] The logic central to human zoos—to show "lesser variation" and thus justify their differential treatment—seemed to echo through media spectacles of racial alterity in the Sydney case via the use of particular exhibitionary strategies deployed in traditional human zoos.[32]

In the first instance, like with human zoos, the inhabitants of these hot spots were *presented in their fenced-off areas*—in this case in an almost endless news cycle. The populace saw imagery of apartment buildings being fenced off or locked down, with residents of one block of fifty apartments in the West, for instance, put under police guard and fourteen days of what a resident characterized as mandatory "imprisonment." The populace saw imagery of cleaners and HAZMAT-suited health workers sanitizing areas deemed infected in these hot spots.[33] They saw media spectacle of police and army containing otherness: patrolling the streets on foot and with road checkpoints, and helicopters monitoring street movement in these areas, alongside imagery of residents under police lockdown being fed by authorities, hanging over balconies, or behind glass

30. Lisa Uddin, *Zoo Renewal: White Flight and the Urban Ghetto* (University of Minnesota Press, 2015), 11.

31. Nigel Rothels, "Aztecs, Aborigines, and Ape-People: Science and Freaks in Germany, 1850–1900," in *Freakery: Cultural Spectacles of the Extraordinary Body,* ed. Rosemary Garland Thomspon (New York University Press, 1996), 160.

32. See Guido Abbattista, "Dehumanizing the Exotic in Living Human Exhibitions," in *The Routledge Handbook of Dehumanization,* ed. Maria Kronfelder (Routledge, 2021).

33. Daniella White, "This Is Imprisonment: Blacktown Apartments in Lockdown After COVID Outbreak," *The Sydney Morning Herald,* July 27, 2021, https://www.smh.com.au/national/nsw/blacktown-apartment-in -lockdown-after-covid-outbreak-20210727-p58d7h.html.

windowpanes because they could not go outside. Such imagery assured viewers that "threatening behavior" had been curtailed.

Alongside and intersecting this first strategy from human zoos was a second: the *rendering of abject humanity for certain groups of people through select imagery or treatment* within their confined environments. This is a *staging to stress difference,* amounting to what L. L. Wynn refers to as "pathological imagery of otherness."[34] Two key examples attest to what we could see as the production of abject humanity of minority groups in the Sydney case. First was the police treatment and media coverage of an "illegal gathering" of members of Christ Embassy Church in Sydney's West, whose Nigerian leader was clearly identified and shown in the media as refusing the lockdown and declaring it over.[35] Authorities took an unprecedented heavy hand, bringing in a police squad team to "break up" the gathering and fining attendees in excess of $35,000. But more than this, the media covered the event by showing the faces of the mainly Black parishioners, one of the only times this was done in reporting on a gathering, and networks circulated historical footage of the church's services. By focusing so intently on this one instance of noncompliance with health orders, the supposed "blackness" of the church was unmistakably marked and singled out as twinned with aberrance and lack of rational deliberation. A second and perhaps more distressing visual example came when police detained a Middle Eastern Australian man (again clearly identified by name and imagery in the media), for not wearing a mask: They handcuffed him on the ground in such a violent manner that paramedics had to revive him with a defibrillator and CPR. He remained hand-

34. L. L. Wynn, "The Pandemic *Imaginerie*: Infectious Bodies and Military-Police Theater in Australia," *Cultural Anthropology* 36, no. 3 (2021): 350–59, 335.

35. Sarah McPhee and Daniella White, "Church and Worshippers Fined $35,000 After 60 People Attend Blacktown Service," *The Sydney Morning Herald,* August 23, 2021, https://www.smh.com.au/national/nsw/church-and-worshippers-fined-35-000-after-60-people-attend-blacktown-service-20210823-p58l64.html.

cuffed throughout the four-minute ordeal.[36] Treatment such as this only confirms perceived lesser status and the maintenance of racial alterity for certain groups—or indeed racialized non/inadequate personhood—especially when juxtaposed with other imagery of scores of carefree people flocking to the golden sands of Bondi and Coogee Beaches outside the zones of concern: In these other (whiter, richer) areas, authorities sanctioned residents to enjoy and breathe the "free air."

A third key strategy of human zoos was also used here, that of those on display being treated as needing to be *led by a white guide or instructor*. In the Sydney case, the media acted as the "showman" or white guide, relaying/interpreting the conditions of lockdown and the actions of hot spot inhabitants to the general populace. State authorities also acted as guides or instructors (who both protected and restrained), imposing the differential restrictions discussed previously. But this perceived requirement was staged in specific ways that compounded the idea that certain groups of people are not only compromised biological citizens—lacking self-government— but persons. For instance, the state health minister, on ABC's *Insight* program, stated there was significant reluctance among what he called large "refugee family groups" with lower incomes to come forward to state health authorities (for contact tracing). "They've suffered greatly in their own nations, in their own countries," he said, continuing that "we are challenged in the south-western suburbs . . . it's a very difficult community to gain the confidence of, and *to have them respond in a way that we need them to* respond."[37]

36. Elizabeth Farrelly, "So Fresh Air Is Good for Seaside Residents but Not LGAs of Concern? Spare Me Your Concern, Mr Hazzard," *The Sydney Morning Herald,* September 17, 2021, https://www.smh.com.au/national /nsw/so-fresh-air-is-good-for-seaside-residents-but-not-lgas-of-concern -spare-me-your-concern-mr-hazzard-20210916-p58seq.html.

37. Natassia Chrysanthos, "Berejklian Launches August Jab Campaign, as Sydney Records 239 New Local Cases," *The Sydney Morning Herald,* August 2, 2021, https://www.smh.com.au/national/nsw/sydney -records-239-new-cases-with-35-infectious-in-the-community-20210801 -p58esl.html (my emphasis).

He compared these communities to those of the (whiter) Northern Beaches Christmas and Eastern suburbs lockdowns that, he said, saw "high level[s] of compliance."[38] He also mentioned how the Muslim community had recently observed Eid, and that noncompliance for such events may lead to further outbreaks.

Through these various examples we see that spectacle created and deployed an "us-vs.-them," "east-vs.-west" reasoning that positions certain people as the "problem." This hierarchical arrangement maintains a clear caesura in the population—a break within what Foucault refers to as "the biological continuum" addressed by biopolitical administration:[39] spectacle governs populations through performing separation.[40] As part of this, spectacle instructs viewers as to their positioning within the biopolitical field: It shapes the attention of those included in the "we," encouraging certain segments of the population to view themselves as somehow exceptional and deserving *against* nondeserving others. Visibility and exposure are *modes* of zoological governance then—where the population is administered along racial lines. But these kinds of spectacle ultimately *materialize* alterity and the supposedly insufficiently human through the production of differential status and value.

Zoo-logos

Within Western culture, racialized groups have long been likened to animals. The standardized view is that these groups of people have been dehumanized, stripped of their human status. But racialized peoples have never been viewed as fully human. The category "human" within Western knowledge systems was always already defined against animality, *and the production of racial difference was*

38. Chrysanthos, "Berejklian Launches."
39. Foucault, *Society Must Be Defended,* 255.
40. Krupar and Ehlers, "The Racial Spectacular."

always tethered to animality and nature.[41] As a taxonomy of power, race divides—with whites taken as the quintessentially human and all non-whites arranged to varying degrees (and shifting in various temporal periods) in a transient space between human and animals. Inseparable from the discourse of speciesism, the production and maintenance of race is thus predicated on *zoo-logos*—a knowledge related to animality[42]—and, as such, *racialization is zoological*. What I have tentatively called zoological governance manages the social sphere according to this logic (zoo-logos) and this operation (racialization as zoological).

In this chapter I have been interested in thinking through these ideas in relation to the pandemic and particularly the Delta outbreak in Sydney. If Covid-19 presented a generalized biosecurity threat to the nation, and biohumanity needed to be protected against this virus, it becomes necessary to ask: Who is the "we" of biohumanity? Clearly, what becomes evident across the empirical terrain of the Sydney case is that those deemed "lesser human" are not protected in the same ways as others and, indeed, that the biosecuritization of health operates according to differential valuations of those within the population—in line with racial difference. More than this, however, certain (racialized) segments of the population were positioned as biological threats to generalized biohumanity and thus in need of specific forms of administration—zoological governance. This selective quarantine did not ameliorate disparities and the overrepresentation of Black and ethnic minority groups in Covid incidence and mortality rates. Instead, health inequalities were undeniably deepened, generating unequal harms. By early 2022, Australian Bureau of Statistic figures on deaths from

41. Claire Jean Kim, *Dangerous Crossings: Race, Species, and Nature in a Multicultural Age* (Cambridge University Press, 2015), 24. Also see Donna Haraway, *Primate Visions: Gender, Race, and Nature in the World of Modern Science* (Routledge, 1989).

42. Claire Jean Kim, "Murder and Mattering in Harambe's House," *Politics and Animals* 3 (2017): 1–15, 10.

Covid noted that those Australians born in North Africa and the Middle East were about ten times more likely to die from the virus than those born in Australia (after age was accounted for). People from Southeast Asia and southern and central Asia recorded twice as many Covid-19 deaths. In distinction, those born in the United Kingdom and Ireland had the lowest death rate.[43]

While this imperiling of minoritized lives is by no means a new story—but centuries old and recursively reiterated in multiple national contexts—the Sydney case highlights particular modalities of zoological governance, specifically as it plays out in the administration of health. Zoological governance manages an always already stratified population. As examined in this chapter, the key technologies deployed in this governance are carcerality (caging) and spectacle (staging), where caging *contains* and seeks to achieve domestication, here a hygenicized reality in the Covid biosecurity calculus, and where staging *fixes* minority racialized populations in selective spectacles of difference, in turn justifying distinct treatment and administration. In this sense, spectacles of racial alterity must also be understood as forms of racial caging.

Zoological governance *targets* racialized groups for *intervention, containment, and subdual.* This is a disciplining of those who are deemed unable to govern themselves. Importantly, however, the function of this disciplinary targeting is not to transform those deemed as other—to normalize—and thus bring them into the fold of the population (a function that is key to carceral society in its generality). Nor is the function to exclude or expel certain subjects from the national populace. Instead, minoritized subjects are *intervened upon to maintain racial order* and the hierarchical relations it entails. Racialized minorities are included—but as lesser beings within the overarching settler-colonial state. They are *conditionally*

43. Stephanie Dalzell, "Government Data Reveals Being Born Overseas Increases Your Risk of Dying from COVID-19 in Australia," *ABCNews,* February 16, 2022, https://www.abc.net.au/news/2022-02-17/abs-data-cald-communities-worse-affected-by-covid-outbreaks/100834104.

incorporated on dominant terms, that is, within a system of population control delineated by race and determined by the enduring white state. Ghassan Hage refers to this operation as a "generalized domestication" predicated on "the fantasy whereby we [white settler subjects] make our existence viable by seeking homeliness [struggling to be at home in the world] through aggression and domination."[44] We might see this as an excluded inclusion, then, where racialized others are included on limited grounds. They are included to the extent that they service the dominant (zoological) order as fulcrum—and constitutive other—to the (category) human. They are included in order to recursively resecure what is positioned as "legitimate authority." And, ultimately they are included in ways that augment a system that instructs the populace as to their position within the order—that is, the order of differential status and value.

44. Ghassan Hage, *Is Racism an Environmental Threat? (Debating Race)* (Polity, 2017), 92.

4. Longed for Still: Antiracism, Uncaging, and Modes of Breathing Together

Anne Pollock

THE THEMATIC OF THE CAGE emerged organically through conversations among this book's coauthors, and we have seen how the caging has been evocatively instantiated at different scales in Anthony Hatch's inquiry into the metabolic cage and in Nadine Ehlers's examination of the racialized lockdown in Sydney. Amade Aouatef M'charek began to posit a conceptual route toward uncaging race, by replacing confidence that we know what it is with curiosity and care. In this concluding chapter, I continue to carry the themes of carcerality and the boundaries of the human that have been explored in different ways in each of the earlier chapters, even as I shift the focus a bit in order to explore other ways in which the racial cage might have *openings*.

First, I consider the elusive and oppressive ideal of the hermetic seal in the context of Covid-19 and the vital breaking of the seal by the Movement for Black Lives. Then, I take a more conceptual turn, considering the etymology and philosophy of "the cage" and the urgency of uncaging, as articulated in an earlier era by Marilyn Frye and Maya Angelou. Finally, I close with a section on refusing despair as we strive to dismantle cages of oppression, and holding on to necessary hope.

2020 Fluorescence of Black Lives Matter and/as Uncaging

As we entered various forms lockdown amid the emergence of the novel coronavirus, there was talk of the necessity, possibility, and desirability of living a "hermetically sealed" life. The ability to reach toward this ideal has been a mark of privilege. For example, in a virtual conversation with Arundhati Roy in May 2020, Naomi Klein called on her progressive audience to reject "the rich declaring independence from the rest of the world, and living a kind of hermetically sealed luxury existence."[1]

The hermetic seal might be understood as a very particular kind of cage. In its technical sense, the term "hermetically sealed" generally refers to a total barrier to touch and air. Many manufactured goods are hermetically sealed in this sense: their final production steps taken in a space that is free of contaminants, and vacuum-packed with airtight packaging to maintain sterility. Examples range from ordinary canned goods to many medical and high-tech products. Yet as engineers of hermeticity note, "all enclosures leak, just at different rates."[2]

It is not possible to actually achieve the total stoppage of airflow, even in the most sterile of contexts. If a container around an inanimate object might come close to hermeticity, the same is not true of any space occupied by human beings. Face masks obviously cannot cut off airflow completely. Sealed hospital rooms would be inaccessible to medical personnel and indeed hostile to the survival of organisms inside that rely on exchanges of oxygen and carbon dioxide. An environment without airflow is, literally, one in which humans (among other animals) cannot live.

1. Naomi Klein and Arundhati Roy, "Into the Portal, Leave No One Behind," Haymarket Books Online event, May 19, 2020, https://www.youtube.com/watch?v=w0NYl_73mHY, 51 mins.

2. K. J. Ely, "Validating Hermeticity in Welded Implantable Medical Devices," in *Joining and Assembly of Medical Materials and Devices,* ed. Y. N. Zhou and M. D. Breyen (Woodhead Publishing, 2013).

Carcerality and the boundaries of the human organism that were being worked through in such intriguing ways in Anthony Hatch's chapter on the metabolic cage in this book are also at stake in the elusive ideal of the hermetic seal in the context of Covid-19. Breathing is pivotal for sustaining life in all its many dimensions, and access to breath has become a powerful metonym for access to life in an era that has seen increased awareness of racial disparities in this respiratory disease on the one hand and the racialized impact of police violence on the other. This is why the phrase "I can't breathe" has emerged as such a powerful characterization of both literal and metaphoric conditions in which Black communities struggle to live in a racist society. As Gabriel O. Apata has powerfully argued, "I can't breathe" is a rallying cry for a historic moment in which "recent forms of racial injustice are characterized by an ongoing process of systemic and structural suffocation."[3]

The differential imposition of suffocation along racialized lines is the primary way in which the boundaries of the human are at stake here. The caging and staging of racialized populations in the carceral milieu of Sydney's Covid lockdown that Nadine Ehlers's chapter in this book so acutely analyzes offers a stark instantiation of how racial inequality can be enacted through spectacular operations of difference and/as dehumanization. If all animals are vulnerable to suffocation, the differential imposition of that suffocation according to race is distinctly human.

There is also an additional way in which this phenomenon operates on the non/human boundary: intentionality in how we respond to that structural suffocation, individually or in community. The insistence that "Black Lives Matter" in a context in which Black lives are pervasively disregarded is continuous with the civil rights–era insistence "I *Am* A Man." The earlier slogan, from the 1968 Memphis sanitation workers strike, had layers: "I *Am* A Man"

3. Gabriel O. Apata, "'I Can't Breathe': The Suffocating Nature of Racism," *Theory, Culture & Society* 37, no. 7–8 (2020): 241–54.

contested the use of the demeaning term *boy* as a term of address for Black men, and it made a claim to human rights in terms of equality and dignity.[4] The slogan "Black Lives Matter," which emerged in 2013 in response to the acquittal of the vigilante killer of Trayvon Martin, extends beyond a masculinist frame. Its reference to "lives" evokes both biology and biography (a pair of *bios* terms that are usefully considered together).[5] In both eras, the stark declarative statements make a compelling demand for inclusion in society.

Here we might remember the etymology of "conspiracy" as "breathing together." In doing so, we wrest the term *conspiracy* from the monopoly of *conspiracy theorists,* to put it toward aspirational ends. In the conclusion of her important work *On Black Breath,* literary scholar Kimberly Bain calls on readers to conspire—Bain chooses "conspire" over "solidarity" because "unlike solidarity (which has no verb form unless transformed by the phrase 'to be in') conspire is in of itself a verb and in of itself demands action."[6] Urgently, Bain argues, "shared breathing" involves "sharing the burden of being at risk," and conspiracy is "about taking on the risks of being vulnerable and open to others and the world, a vulnerability and risk that emerges with breathing and that certain bodies disproportionally absorb."[7]

Bain's work on Black breath is part of a recent fluorescence of theoretical engagement with breath, much of it coming from an environmental justice perspective, exemplified by a Thematic Collection in *Engaging Science, Technology, & Society* on "Breathing Late Industrialism."[8] Anthropologist Tim Choy, in his commentary

4. Steve Estes, *I Am A Man!: Race, Manhood, and the Civil Rights Movement* (University of North Carolina Press, 2005).

5. Alondra Nelson, "Bio Science: Genetic Genealogy Testing and the Pursuit of African Ancestry," *Social Studies of Science* 38, no. 5 (2008): 759–83.

6. Kimberly Bain, *On Black Breath* (Unpublished PhD diss., Princeton University, September 2020), 211–12.

7. Bain, *On Black Breath*, 211–12.

8. Chloe Ahmann and Alison Kenner, "Breathing Late Industrialism," *Engaging Science, Technology, and Society* 6 (2020): 416–38.

"On Breathing Together" in that collection, argues that "the work of drawing breath together entails the proliferation of comparisons, contrasts, and connections."[9] Bringing a critique of the environmental conditions of late industrialism together with the antiracist plea "I can't breathe," Choy argues that the symbolic, theoretical, and material connections that come together in the histories of "respiratory thickening paired incommensurably yet viscerally with linguistic and textual repetitions of racialized respiratory violence."[10]

An urge toward self-suffocation in the face of the risks of breathing together can be powerful but counterproductive. Sometimes a response to the caging of oppressive systems is an effort to build a cage of one's own—for oneself or one's household. We saw this a great deal in the pandemic: seeking to seal oneself off from the outside world as a way to be safe from infection. Thinking with the etymological connection between caging and caring that Amade Aouatef M'charek highlighted in her chapter from a different angle, suffocating confinement could feel like care. Yet living a hermetically sealed life is not only ultimately impossible; it also cuts us off from the possibility to care beyond the borders of the household. If temporary closures might have a utility, as a way of life, their construction and maintenance is antithetical to social justice.

As Black Lives Matter protests took to the streets in the 2020 fluorescence of that movement, they showed what is worth risking in an unjust world, and the necessity of breaking the hermetic seal. Otherwise, the seal threatens to render breath neither worthwhile nor even possible. The act of breathing together can be an act of defying capitalist impulses and resisting total control. Even as we must acknowledge the importance of preventing viral spread, we need porousness, not sterility, in both our domestic and political spheres. Rhythms of inhale and exhale are essential to breathing, itself vital for being, knowing, and resisting. Activism, even in pan-

9. Timothy Choy, "Breathing Together Now," *Engaging Science, Technology, and Society* 6 (2020): 587.

10. Choy, "Breathing Together Now," 586.

demic times, depends on us breathing together. We have to break the seal, and go outside. We cannot forgo breathing together.

Grappling with Racism's Cage

The hermetic seal is just one type of cage, and the fluorescence of the Movement for Black Lives is just one type of uncaging. The examination of the breaking of that seal offers one brightly illuminated perspective onto racial inequality and its contestation, and our analytical view can be enriched by putting this meditation into kaleidoscopic relation with considerations that might be more obscure. Stepping back a bit can help understand additional layers of what is at stake in racism's caging—and the urgent potential for dismantling the cage.

Consider the etymology of the word "cage":

> cage (n.) "box-like receptacle or enclosure, with open spaces, made of wires, reeds, etc.," typically for confining domesticated birds or wild beasts, c. 1200, from Old French *cage* "cage, prison; retreat, hideout" (12c.), from Latin *cavea* "hollow place, enclosure for animals, coop, hive, stall, dungeon, spectators' seats in the theatre" (source also of Italian *gabbia* "basket for fowls, coop;" see cave (n.)). From c. 1300 in English as "a cage for prisoners, jail, prison, a cell."[11]

So, etymologically, caging is enclosing and confining something, but also watching, through openings. Both the closedness and the openness of the cage matter: As they come to be distinguished from each other, a key difference between a cage and a cave is that those outside can see in (to the same extent those inside can see out).

That combination of containment and visibility is why, say, go-go dancers might be in a cage, performing from there for an audience surrounding them in more open spaces. Or "cage fighting"—mixed martial arts, in which the combination of enclosure and exposure

---

11. Online Etymology Dictionary, "Cage," n.d. (accessed January 3, 2023), https://www.etymonline.com/word/cage.

seems to be part of the appeal of the form, while also contributing an animalistic quality to the sport ("human cock fighting"). Although go-go dancers or cage fighters might experience being caged might see the cage as a site of enacting liberation[12] or manhood,[13] being caged is also linked with being dehumanized. There is a tension in these kinds of cagings between physical expression and entrapment. Consider that go-go dancing emerged in the "swinging sixties":

> Unlike dancing with someone else, go-go presented opportunities for greater self-expression, individualism and improvisation. To some extent the dancer's wild gyrations could be interpreted as an energetic response to newfound freedom and a desire for physical expression of the sense of liberation. On the other hand due to the physical containment of girls—whether in cages or on raised podiums, the frantic movements also resemble those of trapped birds, desperate for a way out.[14]

The illusory liberation of women in a sexist society can be seen through and with the cage.

One of the most illuminating theorists of caging as oppression is the philosopher Marilyn Frye, who is writing about primarily sexism rather than racism and yet thinking analogously can be fruitful. In her classic essay on "Oppression," Frye articulates the systematic birdcage of sexism, in which she emphasizes the root of "oppression" as "press," and goes on to use the terminology of caging in order to argue that we need to understand oppression as a structure as a whole rather than just one constraining element: "The experience of oppressed people is that the living of one's life is confined and shaped by forces and barriers which are not accidental or occasional and hence avoidable, but are systematically

12. Georgina Gregory, "Go-Go Dancing—Femininity, Individualism and Anxiety in the 1960s," *Film, Fashion & Consumption* 7, no. 2 (2018): 165–78. https://doi.org/10.1386/ffc.7.2.165_1.

13. Christian A. Vaccaro et al., "Managing Emotional Manhood: Fighting and Fostering Fear in Mixed Martial Arts," *Social Psychology Quarterly* 74, no. 4 (2011): 414–37.

14. Gregory, "Go-Go Dancing," 197.

related to each other in such a way as to catch one between and among them and restrict or penalize motion in any direction. It is the experience of being *caged in*—all avenues, in every direction, are blocked or booby trapped."[15] Frye continues, with a more extended consideration of the cage as a thing to think with:

> Cages. Consider a birdcage. If you look very closely at just one wire in the cage, you cannot see the other wires. If your conception of what is before you is determined by this myopic focus, you could look at that one wire, up and down the length of it, and be unable to see why a bird would not just fly around the wire any time it wanted to go somewhere. Furthermore, even if, one day at a time, you myopically inspected each wire, you still could not see why a bird would have trouble going past the wires to get anywhere. There is no physical property of any one wire, *nothing* that the closest scrutiny could discover, that will reveal how a bird could be inhibited or harmed by it except in the most accidental way.

For Frye, the gaps between the birdcage's wires that make it possible to see the bird in the cage can make it harder to see how the cage operates constrain:

> It is only when you step back, stop looking at the wires one by one, microscopically, and take a macroscopic view of the whole cage, that you can see why the bird does not go anywhere; and then you will see it in a moment. It will require no great subtlety of mental powers. It is perfectly obvious that the bird is surrounded by a network of systematically related barriers, no one of which would be the least hindrance to its flight, but which, by their relations to each other, are as confining as the solid walls of a dungeon.[16]

Frye herself goes on to describe how racism operates in a similarly systematic way to the birdcage of sexism, such that justifications for not being allowed to go to a public space or not being allowed to pursue a preferred line of work might be "because it's not safe

---

15. Marilyn Frye, *The Politics of Reality: Essays in Feminist Theory* (Crossing Press, 1983), 4; emphasis mine.
16. Frye, *The Politics of Reality,* 4–5.

for girls" or because "there's no work for negroes in that line."[17] In either case, "the 'inhabitant' of the 'cage' is not an individual but a group" insofar as "if an individual is oppressed, it is in virtue of being a member of a group or category of people that is systematically reduced, molded, immobilized."[18]

This emphasis on imposition of the cage might spur an additional etymological reflection: The word "cage" is not only a noun but also a verb. To cage is to put into or keep in a cage. Etymologically the verb emerged from the noun: "to confine in a cage, to shut up or confine," 1570s, from cage (n.).[19] This has a distinctly nefarious cast.

The theme of "the cage" is the subject of Black feminist engagement by the African American poet, memoirist, and activist Maya Angelou, who engages with both the oppressive impact of the cage and also the vitality of maintaining imagination in the face of a world that constantly seems to shut imagination down. The title of her first memoir, *I Know Why the Caged Bird Sings,* is an evocative thematic for understanding both the oppressive character of caging and the urgency of uncaging.

I Know Why the Caged Bird Sings, published in 1969, is a gripping account of her childhood experiences of both racism and sexual violence.[20] It is the most prominent of the several autobiographies that Angelou wrote, and was described by her friend and mentor James Baldwin as "a Biblical study of life in the midst of death."[21]

The title of that Angelou autobiography comes from a line from a poem by Paul Lawrence Dunbar (1872–1906), called "Sympathy."[22] Born less than a decade after the end of slavery and writing in the context of the crushing of Reconstruction, Dunbar was the most

17. Frye, 7.

18. Frye, 8.

19. Online Etymology Dictionary, "Cage."

20. Maya Angelou, *I Know Why the Caged Bird Sings* (Virago, 1984 [1969]).

21. Thesslay La Force, "In Memoriam: Maya Angelou, 1928–2014," *Vogue,* May 28, 2014, https://www.vogue.com/article/maya-angelou-in -memoriam.

22. Reprinted in La Force, "In Memoriam."

prominent Black poet of the age.[23] In the iconic poem for which he is most remembered, first published in 1899, Dunbar writes, "I know what the caged bird feels, alas!," and the final stanza "I know why the caged bird beats his wing" culminates:

> I know why the caged bird sings, ah me,
> When his wing is bruised and his bosom sore,—
> When he beats his bars and he would be free;
> It is not a carol of joy or glee,
> But a prayer that he sends from his heart's deep core,
> But a plea, that upward to Heaven he flings—
> I know why the caged bird sings!

Dunbar's caged bird looks to heaven for salvation, whereas Angelou's version is more explicit that the caged bird yearns to fly here on earth. She has her own poem, published much later than the autobiography, which contrasts the free bird with the caged bird in its verses, and its refrain is also its culmination:

> The caged bird sings
> with a fearful trill
> of things unknown
> but longed for still
> and his tune is heard
> on the distant hill
> for the caged bird
> sings of freedom.[24]

Holding onto the capacity to sing of freedom is vital. Yet authentic freedom requires more than merely opening the cage, and for hu-

---

23. Gene Andrew Jarrett, *Paul Laurence Dunbar: The Life and Times of a Caged Bird* (Princeton University Press, 2022).

24. Maya Angelou, *Shaker, Why Don't You Sing?* (Random House, 1983).

man beings, it cannot be achieved on a merely individual level but rather requires being in community. In the antiracism movements from Dunbar's era through to Angelou's and to Black Lives Matter, imagination and community are both vital components of contesting the constraints of racism's cagings.

Imagination and community as liberatory resources are also articulated in the writing of Ruha Benjamin, who is one of the most prominent voices at the intersection of science and technology studies and African American studies today and so a particularly relevant touchstone for this book. The "liberatory imagination" aspect comes to the fore in Benjamin's 2019 edited collection, *Captivating Technology: Race, Carceral Technoscience, and the Liberatory Imagination.* In her introduction to that book, Benjamin engages with the themes of carcerality and with its contestation when she argues that "technology captivates" in two different ways: "capturing bodies" in the prison industrial complex and pervasive structures of carcerality and control; but also "capturing the imagination" in ways that can be, potentially, toward a liberatory imagination: "Ferguson is the future" and beyond.[25] This dual aspect of how technology captivates offers an evocative engagement with the racism's caging and aspirations toward uncaging.

Attention to the persistence of the liberatory imagination in the face of oppression becomes even more central to Ruha Benjamin's 2022 book, *Viral Justice,* and that book also foregrounds the importance of connecting with community to contest injustice.[26] One of that book's most striking features is that it not only names injustices that need to end but also names what it wants to see more of, including gardens among other places for fostering and cultivating necessary sustenance. There are many beautiful examples given of people living *viral justice,* including the "gangsta gardener,"

25. Ruha Benjamin, ed., *Captivating Technology: Race, Carceral Technoscience, and the Liberatory Imagination* (Duke University Press, 2019).

26. Ruha Benjamin, *Viral Justice: How We Build the World We Want* (Princeton University Press, 2022).

the Critical Resistance Anti-Policing Health Toolkit, Black doulas and midwives, and more.

These inspiring endeavors that Benjamin calls our attention to all illuminate the ways in which science, technology, and medicine are circuits not only of power and inequality but also of social justice movements that resist them.[27] In a usefully grounded and concrete way, the activists who Benjamin draws our attention to exemplify *prefigurative politics,* which is to say that these activists embody and enact, within their activism, the socialities and practices they seek to foster for broader society.[28] We live in an unjust world and no amount of work in our communities can evade that, and yet that is not a reason to let the unjust structures of the larger world set the terms of all of our relationships. As scholars and as activists, we can and should hold onto hope.

Necessary Hope

"Hope" is a common word, and yet a complicated concept. I have explored this before with regard to postcolonial science projects,[29] and it is no less relevant for articulating antiracisms. Indeed, hope is an essential part of struggles for social justice, including anti-racist social movements. As the educator and philosopher Paulo Freire argues:

> I am hopeful not out of mere stubbornness, but out of an existen-
> tial, concrete imperative. I do not mean that, because I am hopeful,
> I attribute to this hope of mine the power to transform reality all by
> itself, so that I set out for the fray without taking account of concrete,

27. Cf. Anne Pollock and Banu Subramaniam, "Resisting Power, Retooling Justice: Promises of Feminist Postcolonial Technosciences," *Science, Technology, & Human Values* 41, no. 6 (2016): 951–66.

28. Guilherme Moreira Fians, "Prefigurative Politics," *The Cambridge Encyclopedia of Anthropology,* 2022. https://doi.org/10.29164 /22prefigpolitics.

29. Anne Pollock, *Synthesizing Hope: Matter, Knowledge, and Place in South African Drug Discovery* (University of Chicago Press, 2019).

material data, declaring "My hope is enough!" No, my hope is necessary, but it is not enough. Alone, it does not win. But without it, my
struggle will be weak and wobbly. We need critical hope the way a
fish needs unpolluted water.[30]

Thus, hope does not let us off the hook, but rather means that we
have work to do. Freire's metaphorical reference here to the fish's
need for water is resonant with the theme of breath that has per-
meated this chapter. The water for the fish and analogous critical
hope for us is necessary for both oxygen and forward movement.

Cheryl Mattingly makes an aligned argument that hope can be
usefully understood "as a *practice,* rather than simply an emotion
or a cultural attitude."[31] So hope here is not merely optimism, even
as it is a refusal to submit to pessimism. Cheryl Mattingly also ac-
knowledges that, "paradoxically, hope is on intimate terms with
despair. It asks for more than life promises."[32] Hope is an engine
on which capitalism operates, but it is also something more than its
entrepreneurial elements. Our awareness of the pitfalls of hope is
not a reason to abandon it. I think that we sometimes use pessimism
to protect ourselves from disappointment. There can be a small
satisfaction in having correctly predicted how bad things would be.
But failing to cultivate hope inhibits our ability to engage creatively
with the world—whether through poetry, activism, or otherwise.

Note that living with hope is also different from what Lauren
Berlant has indicted as "cruel optimism," which is when something that we desire is actually an obstacle to our flourishing—for
example, in the longing for "the American Dream" that many are
doomed to fail to achieve.[33] Like that dream, the hope that progres-
sives also need involves longing for something that we will never

30. Paulo Freire, *Pedagogy of Hope: Reliving "Pedagogy of the
Oppressed,"* trans. Robert R. Barr (Bloomsbury Academic, 2014 [1968]).

31. Cheryl Mattingly, *The Paradox of Hope: Journeys Through a Clinical
Borderland* (University of California Press, 2010), 6.

32. Mattingly, *The Paradox of Hope,* 6.

33. Lauren Berlant, *Cruel Optimism* (Duke University Press, 2011).

actually reach, but unlike that dream, it is doing so terms beyond the neoliberal entrepreneurial subject.

Indeed, the hope we need is necessarily in opposition to the American Dream. In her article "Caretaking Relations, Not American Dreaming," Kim TallBear decries pervasive Indigenous erasure even as she embraces Junot Díaz's idea of "radical hope," which puts "trust in the collective genius of all the people who have survived these wicked systems . . . I think from the bottom will the genius come that makes our ability to live with each other possible."[34] TallBear embraces this kind of hope as absolutely necessary: "I will myself to have this kind of radical hope. What is the alternative?"[35] Later in the piece, TallBear aligns herself with Cornel West's "multiracial alliance" even as she also goes beyond it, both because he himself too often participates in Indigenous erasure and because that multiracial alliance does not go far enough: "I stand in alliance with relatives—both human and other-than-human—who suffer across the planet from the violence that is the American Dream."[36]

Like TallBear I am well aware of Cornel West's shortcomings, and yet the hope that I believe that we need to foster is rooted in what Cornel West has beautifully characterized as "prophetic pragmatism":

> Prophetic pragmatism is a form of tragic thought in that it confronts candidly individual and collective experiences of evil in individuals and institutions—with little expectation of ridding the world of all evil. Yet it is a kind of romanticism in that it holds many experiences of evil to be neither inevitable nor necessary, but rather the results of human agency, i.e. choices and actions. This interplay between tragic thought and romantic impulse, inescapable evils and transformable evils makes prophetic pragmatism seem schizophrenic. On the one hand, it appears to affirm a Sisyphean outlook in which human re-

---

34. Junot Díaz, quoted in Kim TallBear, "Caretaking Relations, Not American Dreaming," *Kalfou* 6, no. 1 (2019): 34.

35. Tallbear, "Caretaking Relations," 34.

36. TallBear, 38.

sistance to evil makes no progress. On the other hand, it looks as if it approves a utopian quest for paradise. In fact, prophetic pragmatism denies Sisyphean pessimism and utopian perfectionism. Rather, it promotes the possibility of human progress and the impossibility of human paradise.[37]

Hope need not be a hope for a utopia; there can and should be hope for a better world. Holding onto necessary hope, we might return to the theme of breath: in medicine, *aspiration* is the action or process of drawing breath, and in our social world, it is essential to liberation.

Taking advantage of the fact that we can see glimpses of freedom through the wires of racism's cage, we need to hold onto a liberatory imagination. Even after taking account of so many interlocking injustices that antiracism scholarship illuminates—or perhaps especially after doing so—we need to think and act as if it is possible to open the cage.

Acknowledgments

In addition to being deeply informed by extended conversations with the coauthors of this volume and feedback on a presentation at the Sydney Centre for Healthy Societies, this chapter owes a deep debt to Nassim Parvin, who was my original interlocutor on the topic of the hermetic seal.

37. Cornel West, "On Prophetic Pragmatism," in *The Cornel West Reader* (Basic Books, 1999), 166.

Coda

AS WE DRAW THIS SHORT BOOK to a close, we are not in the same place where we started, and yet the journey is not finished. The bio, the human, and race all remain unsettled objects of analysis, and indeed we hope that these concepts feel more open-ended than they did when we began, rather than more closed down.

Recall that we opened with Anna Tsing's injunction to "look around" rather than ahead,[1] and that still holds even after having looked through four turns of the kaleidoscope that has refracted the racial cage. In each of the chapters, we have asked how we might do difference differently. We have questioned how looking at difference through a biohumanities lens might shift the boundaries between the human and more than human. If biohumanities—as we've seen unfold through these chapters—takes a (posthuman) humanities approach to question what we mean by the "human" as a based point, it might enable us to consider how the very idea of the human and human-centered social and cultural life contours biological life, and how this is racialized. In relation to these ideas, we have looked around on multiple levels, drawing on sources in the history of science and contemporary media and policy reports, as well as philosophy and poetry. By engaging in a

1. Anna Lowenhaupt Tsing, *The Mushroom at the End of the World* (Princeton University Press, 2015).

work-in-progress biohumanities approach that has taken neither the bio not the human for granted, our curiosity has been piqued rather than satisfied by this process.

Holding onto this open-endedness in our inquiry into race is an essential aspect of the contestation of the carcerality of race. As we continue to confront new cagings, we will also be on the lookout for new dismantlings.

Acknowledgments

The research for this book has many origin points and is a result of long conversations between the authors, across continents and time. We first began our discussions many years ago now at King's College London, made possible through a Wellcome Trust Small Grant, "Race and Biomedicine Beyond the Lab." While we continued our connections in research over the ensuing years, this book is a product, at least in part, due to us coming together under the auspices of the Sydney Centre for Healthy Societies at the University of Sydney, where we have been leading a research theme on "Race, Ethnicity, and the Biohumanities." We thank the Centre for bringing us together in this way and for providing the initial provocation to explore the ideas that became this book. Jason Weideman welcomed the project at the University of Minnesota Press, and we would like to thank him for his support and conviction in regard to the ideas we explore. The insights of an anonymous reviewer helped crystallize our thinking, and we appreciate their intellectual generosity.

Anthony extends special thanks to his partners at Black Box Labs at Wesleyan University for their ongoing research on metabolism cages and to Suzanne Gottschang and Kathleen Pierce for providing the protective institutional support and rich intellectual community he needed to develop this book while appointed as the William Allan Neilson Chair of Research at Smith College.

Anne, in addition to being deeply informed by extended conversations with the coauthors of this volume and feedback on a presentation at the Sydney Centre for Healthy Societies, owes a great debt to Nassim Parvin, who was her original interlocutor on the topic of the hermetic seal.

Amade thanks her coauthors for an exceptional process of thinking and writing together that led to this book, and in particular Nadine Ehlers for guiding us gently and keeping us on track. Amade also thanks the RaceFaceID team for constant conversations on race and science, and the European Research Council for generously funding her research into race and forensics through a Consolidator Grant (FP7-617451-RaceFaceID); see also https://race-face-id.eu.

Nadine would like to thank her coauthors. The conversations that led to this book, in all their many forms over the years, have been sustaining and always challenging in the best possible ways.

(Continued from page iii)

Forerunners: Ideas First

Matthew J. Wolf-Meyer
Theory for the World to Come: Speculative Fiction and Apocalyptic Anthropology

Nicholas Tampio
Learning versus the Common Core

Kathryn Yusoff
A Billion Black Anthropocenes or None

Kenneth J. Saltman
The Swindle of Innovative Educational Finance

Ginger Nolan
The Neocolonialism of the Global Village

Joanna Zylinska
The End of Man: A Feminist Counterapocalypse

Robert Rosenberger
Callous Objects: Designs against the Homeless

William E. Connolly
Aspirational Fascism: The Struggle for Multifaceted Democracy under Trumpism

Chuck Rybak
UW Struggle: When a State Attacks Its University

Clare Birchall
Shareveillance: The Dangers of Openly Sharing and Covertly Collecting Data

la paperson
A Third University Is Possible

Kelly Oliver
Carceral Humanitarianism: Logics of Refugee Detention

P. David Marshall
The Celebrity Persona Pandemic

Davide Panagia
Ten Theses for an Aesthetics of Politics

David Golumbia
The Politics of Bitcoin: Software as Right-Wing Extremism

Sohail Daulatzai
Fifty Years of *The Battle of Algiers*: Past as Prologue

Gary Hall
The Uberfication of the University

Mark Jarzombek
Digital Stockholm Syndrome in the Post-ontological Age

Nadine Ehlers is associate professor of sociology at the University of Sydney and the author of *Racial Imperatives: Discipline, Performativity, and Struggles Against Subjection,* coauthor of *Deadly Biocultures: The Ethics of Life-Making* (Minnesota, 2019), and coeditor of *Subprime Health: Race and Debt in U.S. Medicine* (Minnesota, 2017).

Anthony Ryan Hatch is professor of science and technology studies at Wesleyan University, with affiliations in African American studies, environmental studies, and sociology. He is the author of *Blood Sugar: Racial Pharmacology and Food Justice in Black America* (Minnesota, 2016) and *Silent Cells: The Secret Drugging of Captive America* (Minnesota, 2019).

Amade Aouatef M'charek is professor of anthropology of science in the Department of Anthropology at the University of Amsterdam. She is the author of *The Human Genome Diversity Project: An Ethnography of Scientific Practice* and coeditor of *Law, Practice and Politics of Forensic DNA Profiling: Forensic Genetics and Their Technolegal Worlds.*

Anne Pollock is professor of global health and social medicine at King's College London. She is the author of three books: *Medicating Race: Heart Disease and Durable Preoccupations with Difference*; *Synthesizing Hope: Matter, Knowledge, and Place in South African Drug Discovery*; and *Sickening: Anti-Black Racism and Health Disparities in the United States* (Minnesota, 2021).